A Chronicle of Small Beer

A Chronicle of Small Beer

The memoirs of a Victorian actress

Winifred Dolan

Edited by

Andy Moreton

STR
The Society *for*
Theatre Research

Society for Theatre Research
London

First published in 2010
by the Society for Theatre Research
PO Box 53971
London, SW15 6UL

ISBN 978 0 85430 077 8

General Editor: Professor Richard Foulkes

Volume Editor: Katherine Newey

Printed and bound by CPI Antony Rowe, Chippenham, Wiltshire

Contents

List of Illustrations

Foreword

by Katherine Newey

Winifred Dolan is rarely mentioned in the many biographies and autobiographies of those who feature so largely in her story. Nor is her life and work mentioned in studies of *fin de siècle* London theatre. She is an invisible woman, brought to life now by Andy Moreton's canny eye, and the Victoria and Albert's custodianship of her theatrical ephemera. As Andy Moreton declares in his preface, Winifred Dolan captures the reader with her artless prose, and her narrative of the great stars and powerful personalities of the London West End in the heyday of the actor-manager satisfy a love of gossip which we can (sometimes) dignify as 'theatre history'.

Yet this memoir offers so much more than gossip, although gossip itself is the stuff of which theatrical legend is made. It *is* theatre history, and an important part of it, at that. Its evidence of the life of a 'jobbing' actor, rather than a star is precious, all the more so, because the memoir is preserved as part of a larger personal collection. Winifred Dolan tells us about the punishing schedule of touring, even in the comparative comfort of chartered trains, and speedy communications. She offers detail of ways actors found jobs, learned roles, and what they actually did in their daily work. Her account of her secretaryship to George Alexander is exhausting just to read, let alone imagining how Dolan might actually have managed to survive that punishing routine – and for such a low salary. Dolan is also interesting in her seemingly tangential references to the ways in which the theatre profession intersected with other areas of British public life. On the role of the theatre – the Profession, as she calls it, after Irving taught her to – in the public sphere, her discussion is deliberate, and her defence stout. She offers personal testimony for the gentlemanliness of Henry Irving, and the grace and fine manners of Ellen Terry, and overall, for their contributions to English culture. She barely mentions the scandal of Oscar Wilde (whose manuscript of *The Importance of Being Earnest* she typed), and makes it quite clear where she stood in the whole matter of 'The Maiden Tribute of Modern Babylon'. In the legitimate theatre, Dolan tells us several times, these matters of morality were not relevant.

Dolan's sensitivity to late Victorian concerns about class distinctions and religious allegiances reminds us of priorities in the past which we may no longer share, or even recognise. Her enduring affection for Clement Scott, for example, in spite of his outrageous statements about women working in the theatre in 1898, demonstrates the strength of loyalties of religious sect and creed which are easy to overlook a half century later. Her account of performing at Balmoral Castle stands alongside official records, and subsequent historians' discussions, as a rare insider's account of what it felt like to perform at Balmoral, and how the rituals of royalty affected an ordinary subject. Dolan offers a relatively informal and even ambivalent view of a subject's encounter with her monarch. Her expression of a subject's awe in the presence of Queen Victoria, and her avowed loyalty to the crown, are mixed together with her clear belief in her right to exercise of freedom of religious worship, in spite of her fear that this could be seen as direct disobedience to the monarch's wishes. Winifred Dolan's emphasis on the importance of her spiritual life over her career could be seen as an effect of her life-long life connection with a religious order, an impress of her situation when writing in 1949, on her recollections of her past. However, her memoir suggests her actions were deliberate and resolute even under pressure as a young working woman, rather than as a writer in later life framed by her later circumstances.

Dolan's apparently artless account of her working life in *fin de siècle* London is captivating. It feels fresh – as if recollected in a daily journal, rather than almost fifty years after events. Yet she has her axes to grind, and I suspect that her memoir was not an artless composition, but an attempt to justify much of her subsequent life as a working woman. Two related themes emerge as enduring concerns: the respectability of 'the Profession', and the role of women within it. These have been topics of constant discussion in histories of the theatre, and biographies of theatre practitioners, and Dolan's memoir offers valuable evidence for our continuing fascination with the often sensational intersection of sex, performance, and money. Winifred Dolan's repeated insistence on her respectability is striking. It is a defence against the kind of blanket condemnation of actresses which Clement Scott made in that ill-judged essay of 1898: 'It is really impossible for a woman to remain pure who adopts the stage as a profession.' Scott said nothing original: he drew on 200 years of equating actresses with prostitutes, assisted by familiar stories of orange sellers, and duke's mistresses. All these stories overlook the hard work and professional performance skills of these memorialised actresses. And that is Dolan's point: while being paid far less than a man, she did a man's work, with competence and efficiency, often teaching those paid more than her. Hers is the story of many a personal assistant, or nurse, or other feminised 'helpmeet' who saves her boss's reputation. Dolan's story is a refreshing reminder of what women – even invisible women – achieved in a period when playwriting, producing, and managing in the theatre were seen as innately masculine activities.

Dolan was not alone. Other autobiographies and memoirs of the period emphasise the respectability of actresses, and their poor treatment in the industry. Indeed, the rhetorical push of the suffrage and suffragette movements was based on the innate respectability of women, particularly of working women. And Dolan was living through a period typified in the press and in art as the period of the 'New Woman'. The woman who never married, got a good education, worked, and kept her own establishment. Vivie Warren and Nora Helmer were the fictional models of this New Woman, but of course, as Dolan shows us, the reality was both more complicated, and less freighted with moral absolutes in the real lives of individuals. Her near contemporary, Netta Syrett, vigorously resisted any defeatist story of the sufferings of late Victorian female dependence. Syrett remembered that in the 1880s, 'educated girls of any character [...] were asserting their right to independence,' and that 'so long as a girl was working at some art, profession, or business, she was perfectly free, and could go about her lawful occasions without censure—even from the censorious.'[1]

---

[1] *The Sheltering Tree*, (London: Geoffrey Bles, 1939), 5–6, 90. However, Syrett fell foul of Clement Scott's censorious views on women in the theatre in his *Daily Telegraph* review of her prize-winning play, *The Finding of Nancy*. See Katherine Newey, *Women's Theatre Writing in Victorian Britain* (Basingstoke: Palgrave Macmillan, 2005), 29–33.

Foreword

Winifred Dolan's personal archive, now held in the Theatre Collection of the Victoria and Albert Museum, contains more than this carefully prepared memoir. There are still treasures to be discovered through an examination of the whole Dolan collection and many questions left to be asked and answered. The reasoning behind Winifred Dolan's careful collection of the records of her theatrical career bear further investigation.[2] What might have motivated Dolan to write her account of these ten years of her life, and not those dedicated to the Women's Unionist Association, and her subsequent political work? The infection of the theatre runs deep it seems, even in the most unknown and unlikely places.

Katherine Newey
University of Birmingham

---

[2] I am indebted here to discussions with Dr Lucie Sutherland, University of Nottingham, who is researching Winifred Dolan's archive as part of her preparation of a critical biography of George Alexander.

Editor's Preface

Andy Moreton

I first came across the name Winifred Dolan in an auction catalogue at the end of 2004.

It was for Christie's film and entertainment sale, which is traditionally held in London just before Christmas every year. This auction is heavily biased towards the golden age of Hollywood and television, but in the tiny theatre section was Lot 86, 'a quantity of material collected by actress Winifred Dolan'.

Miss Dolan was competing for attention that day with such heavyweight celebrities as Charlie Chaplin, Laurel and Hardy, and Marlene Dietrich. My own interest was in a letter signed by Chico Marx, but I remained intrigued by the Dolan bits and pieces and by what was clearly a close and personal association she'd enjoyed with Henry Irving and Ellen Terry.

Prospective buyers are allowed to examine any item prior to a sale, so I requested a look at Lot 86 and three capacious boxes were duly brought out from under the table. They were overflowing with all kinds of memorabilia relating to Winifred Dolan's career during the last ten years of the nineteenth century: personal letters, signed photographs, programmes, annotated scripts and much else besides. As I rummaged further, I came across a chunky, hard-back unlined book containing her memoirs. Everything had been meticulously written in beautiful script in black ink, with relevant newspaper cuttings and a variety of illustrations pasted in. A brief flick through left me fascinated, not least because of the names that kept leaping off the page: Sarah Bernhardt, Oscar Wilde, Lillie Langtry, even Queen Victoria herself. The writing style was polished and assured, the backstage gossip a joy. I very much wanted to bid for the memoirs, but I simply didn't have the room to transport or store all the rest of the paraphernalia.

It would be fair to say that the Dolan collection did not set the auction alight - indeed, the hammer came down at a price below the estimate. The room was still buzzing from the sale of a Chaplin walking cane for £40,000. As fate would have it, while waiting to settle up for the Marx letter for which I'd bid successfully, I overheard the man in front of me in the queue paying for Lot 86. We fell into conversation. 'What on earth are you going to do with it all?' I asked. 'It's no problem,' he replied, 'I represent the Theatre Museum.'

At that time, the museum was in its original home in the Covent Garden area of Central London. It later closed, to re-appear as the V&A Theatre Collections at the Victoria and Albert Museum.

The museum's extensive written archives are available to researchers at Blythe House, an old office building hidden away in west London, and it was there, on Valentine's Day 2007, that Winifred truly stole my heart. That was when I finally had the chance to read in full the little book I'd browsed through at Christie's.

I found a story, told with humour and honesty, of life in front of and behind the curtain – first at one of the last of the Victorian repertory companies and then at one of the top London theatres at a time when the actor-manager was still king … although for not much longer. There was also a snapshot of the social scene in the 1890s as Britain approached the end of Queen Victoria's long reign to usher in the Edwardian era.

What I found particularly appealing was that, unlike most theatrical reminiscences, this was not a story of prize-winning performances in front of adoring audiences. This was about honest endeavour and ultimate failure. Winifred Dolan did not make the grade as a leading actress; she was unable to break into the male-dominated world of producing (to which she herself later felt that she might have been better suited); and, as a playwright, it was a case of nearly but not quite. I don't know whether Miss Dolan kept a contemporaneous diary, but her recall of events, dates and even conversations is remarkably detailed. For someone who once understudied five leading roles and three minor ones at the same time, however, committing lines to memory was presumably never a problem.

In editing these memoirs, I have kept to Winifred Dolan's words as closely as possible, only carefully re-writing to clarify a point or to use a synonym where a word has become outmoded. The idea of having a Shakespearean quote to introduce each chapter and sum up that part of her life came from her.

I'm obliged to Jim Fowler, Head of Collections Development and Research at V&A Theatre Collections (the man in the queue at Christie's), and Guy Baxter, formerly Archivist and Conservation Manager, for allowing us to bring this story to a wider audience. Amy King, Assistant Curator, was a great help with photography and copyright matters. Thanks, also, to the rest of the staff at the reading room at Blythe House, where I spent many pleasant hours.

I'm sincerely grateful, too, to the Canonesses of the Holy Sepulchre in England. Winifred Dolan lived happily with the Community at New Hall in Chelmsford for nearly forty years and left it all her effects. The Community's decision – after much soul-searching – to put up some of these for auction in 2004 has meant that those with an interest in late Victorian theatre have before them a new and fascinating insight from someone who was there.

The Prioress, Sister Teresa, and the archivist, Sister Mary Magdalene, helped me to build up a picture of Winifred Dolan's life after 1920. Sister Mary Therese and Sister Stephanie kindly recounted their recollections of being taught by Winifred Dolan at New Hall during the last war and these are contained in my Epilogue.

I'm grateful to Tony Tuckwell for permission to quote from his book *New Hall and its School* (Free Range Publishing, 2006). David Rankin and Michael Wheatley-Ward are keeping the name of Winifred Dolan's first professional mentor alive with the Sarah Thorne Theatre Club at Broadstairs in Kent and they kindly provided me with information and pictures of Miss Thorne and the Theatre Royal. I'd also like to thank Geoff Morley, Sam Moreton, Peggy Schoonhoven, Barbara Drysdale, Frances Line and Ann Gregory, who all read the manuscript and offered helpful suggestions and encouragement. It's been a great pleasure working with the Society For Theatre Research and I thank Professor Richard Foulkes for nursing the project along; Amy Myers, who did so much to prepare the text for publication, and, of course, Katherine Newey, who put Winifred Dolan's story into context in her excellent foreword, and whose expertise was invaluable in developing the footnotes.

Andy Moreton,
Harrow.

Prologue

'I will a round unvarnish'd tale deliver'
– Othello

Long ago, Mother Mary Magdalen (Falls) and some other nuns urged me to write an account of my life on the stage. At the time, I refused. But now that I am a very old woman, I find I can look back across the chasm of 60 years with a curious degree of detachment – as though the story were that of another person I once knew.

So here it is, such as it is. The stage today is so utterly different from the stage I knew that possibly the perspective of time may lend it an interest it could not claim for itself as 'A Chronicle of Small Beer'.

Winifred M. Dolan,
New Hall,
Chelmsford, Essex.
May 1949.

Chapter I

'There was a star danced, and under that was I born'
– Much Ado About Nothing

I think I have always had the stage in my blood.

Where I got it from I don't know, but it seems obvious it was there because I wrote my first play when I was eight years old. I knew nothing whatever about the theatre except that I can just remember staying with Aunt Mary in Eccleston Square, London, and being taken with the little cousins to the pantomime.

That must have been at Drury Lane around 1873, but as I was only about six years old, all I can remember about it is that the subject was Little Bo-Peep, there were real sheep (with which I was delighted) and a terrible dragon (at which I was terrified).

I had a little playmate two years younger than myself. She was Margaret England, the niece of Mr Allbutt and his wife, who lived quite near to us in Leeds.[1] It was Margaret who was destined to play my first leading lady.

The title of my play was *Rosabella,* and the characters just He and She. It was written in rhyme and was in two acts. In Act I 'they meet' and 'it is raining cats and dogs'. He has an umbrella; she has not. Only a few lines have lingered in my memory, but they were the opening ones and launched the plot with a directness from which the initiated could easily prophesy the dénouement.

> He: O lovely Rosabella
> You have no umbrella!
>
> She: I care not for one
> Them I always shun!
>
> He: Do you like cheese? (She takes offence)
> Don't be angry, please.
>
> She: Don't be so rude!
>
> He: What, in an angry mood?
>
> (She walks off, nose in air. He faints. Curtain.)

All I can remember about the reconciliation in Act II are the lines that ended the play:

> Both: Hark! The marriage bells are ringing
> To us many blessings bringing.

---

[1] Probably Dr (later Sir) Clifford Allbutt (1836–1925), a leading physician in Leeds and inventor of the clinical thermometer. He is generally regarded as the model for Dr Lydgate in George Eliot's *Middlemarch*.

1

It proved an unexpected triumph. At regular intervals, Margaret and I were whisked off to friends' houses to 'do our little play'. I was enchanted, but Margaret was bored – indeed, she had all the temperament proper for a leading lady. Drunk with success, I decided to write another play and talked it over with my mother:

Me:	Mama!
Mrs D:	Well?
Me:	I've been thinking. You know people don't talk in verse in real life…
Mrs D:	Yes.
Me:	In my next play I am going to make them talk as we do.
Mrs D:	In prose.
Me:	No, not in prose – just straight on, you know.
Mrs D:	That is prose.

Thus I learned that I had been speaking prose all my life. What a revelation! The next play, then, was written in that form. It was called *The Knight's Return*; the characters were A Knight and His Lady and, like *Rosabella,* it was in two acts.

In the first, I – the Knight – go off to the Crusades, comforting my Lady with the honour and glory my deeds would bring her. In the next Act, my Lady is a widow, but I return, disguised as a palmer,[2] 'to break the news gently lest joy should kill'. I recite in the third person all that 'he' has achieved in the way of the promised glory. Then, at the right moment, I throw off my palmer's cloak and, my Lady having duly recognised me, we embrace.

Now, according to dramatic convention, the play should have ended there. But alas, necessity drove me against my instinct to consent to an anti-climax. The problem was, you see, that Margaret had refused to accept the part of my Lady – 'There's far too much to learn!' In vain, I cut and cut and cut until there was practically only my own part left and all Margaret had to do was nod yes or no. Still the minx was obdurate. She preferred to play with her dolls and hated acting. Well, if it came to that, I hated dolls … but they gave me an idea.

'If I bring your dolls into the play, will you act the Lady?' I asked. Margaret consented and that was that. But how was I to introduce them? I was determined she should have only one line and Margaret learned it – indeed, Sarah Bernhardt herself[3] could not have spoken it better. It brought the house down and quite stole my thunder. This was it:

(After the embrace)

Lady:	And I, too, have not been idle (drawing back a curtain to reveal seven dolls, one of them black). Come and look at all my little children!

---

[2] A mediaeval Christian pilgrim – generally from western Europe – who carried a palm leaf as a token of having visited the Holy Land.
[3] Sarah Bernhardt (1844–1923), French actress, one of the great theatrical figures of the day.

1. 'A little faded now': the photo bought by a star-struck Winifred Dolan in Leeds in 1879.
   (V&A Images/Theatre Collections)

I was hurt to tears by the hysterical laughter which always greeted the fall of the curtain. In vain, I implored my mother to tell me why they were so amused. She wisely left it to time to solve the riddle.

This perplexing amusement spread, for the family told my uncle, Alfred Austin[4] and he told Henry Irving, who related it to Ellen Terry,[5] until many years later it was actually told to me in the dressing room at the St James's Theatre by an actress – a cousin of the Earl of Dartmouth – at whose table she'd heard it! But when it reached the distinction of being quoted by Lord Peter Wimsey in print ('I, too, have not been idle, as the lady said') it was the last straw. I was not going to be robbed forever of the authorship of that immortal line. I wrote to Miss Dorothy L. Sayers and had a very charming letter in reply. As for Margaret, she married the Dean of Trinity College, Cambridge.

In 1876, I went to school. The Leeds Girls' High School had been started by a committee of ladies and gentlemen interested in education. Several friends of the family were on the committee and they persuaded my mother to let me become a day pupil at the new school. My sister, Aggie, who was ten years older than I, had been educated at Roehampton and New Hall in the south of England, but by the time I was school-ripe, we had suffered financial reverses and boarding school at a convent was beyond the family purse.[6] So, with great reluctance, I was sent to the strictly non-denominational school, trusting myself to counterbalance any damage to my Catholic religion.

And then, at last, came the realisation of my heart's desire to see a real play acted at a theatre. The Grand Theatre in Leeds, which had opened towards the end of 1878, was presenting *Jane Shore*.[7] Somebody had sent my mother some tickets and, of course, my grown-up sister would be attending with my parents. In vain I begged to be allowed to go too, until my sister said: 'Oh let her come, she won't understand a word of it!'

So I went – deeply wounded in my dignity but swallowing insult to attain my desire. Alas, it was a true word my sister had spoken: I could not make head nor tail of the plot and when Gloucester was accused of causing Jane Shore's hand to wither, I asked: 'Is it really hurt?', and was told 'Hush, no.' It was strong meat for a child to digest and frankly I was bitterly disappointed with my first 'real' play.

Later on in 1879, I heard my elders talking of a Mr Irving and Miss Ellen Terry who were coming to Leeds in the course of a provincial tour from the Lyceum Theatre in London. My brother, Ossie, and my cousin, Harry, decided to go and see them from the pit.[8] I implored my parents to let me go too and as the play was *Hamlet* and I was nearly twelve, permission was given.

I forget where I had been that morning, but when I came home, I found that they'd had an early luncheon and had left without me. My disappointment was so devastating that I actually got my mother to let me run after them to try to catch them up.

---

[4] The English poet Alfred Austin (1835–1913), who succeeded Tennyson as Poet Laureate in 1896. He was the brother of Winifred Dolan's mother, also a Winifred.

[5] Henry Irving (1838–1905) and Ellen Terry (1847–1928), the foremost theatrical partnership of the day.

[6] In the census of 1871, Winifred Dolan's father, John C. Dolan, had described himself as 'a woollen manufacturer employing 179 hands'. By the census of 1881, the business had evidently gone and he was employed as an insurance agent.

[7] *The Tragedy of Jane Shore,* a play about the mistress of Edward IV, written by Nicholas Rowe in 1714, professedly in imitation of Shakespeare's style. The Grand had opened on 18 November 1878 with Wilson Barrett as actor-manager. The first production was Shakespeare's *Much Ado About Nothing*.

[8] The cheaper seats in a theatre – consisting of benches occupying the space nearest the stage.

'Now remember,' she said, 'if you don't find the boys you are to come back.' She gave me half-a-crown and I promised. How I ran! The tail end of the waiting crowd was jostling its way in (there were no queues in those days, you just scrimmaged) … but no sight of the boys. They must have secured a place well forward and were already inside. I wormed my way through the crush and presented my nose at the little pay-window.

'Please, if I can find my brother who has just gone in, I am allowed to stay. But if I don't,' (a gasp) 'I must go home again. Can I have my money back if I can't find my brother inside?' The very audacity of the proposal – and perhaps the Yorkshireman's sense of thrift – must have done the trick, for the dear man said, 'All right, luv.' And I paid my money and went in.

The pit was already three-quarters full, the rows packed and there, in the very middle at the front, sat Harry and Ossie. How could I reach them? My conscience told me it was understood that I should be in their company. The orange seller walking up and down the gangway hawking her wares caught sight of me standing there looking lost. 'What is it?' she asked. I opened my heart to her and with a 'Come on, luv' I was taken by the arm down to the front row. The people were told to 'let the lass pass to her brother yonder', which they did (oh, the camaraderie of the pit!). I was just in time to see the curtain go up.

I must confess I did not understand *Hamlet* much better than I had *Jane Shore* but oh, the difference! I could follow the emotions without realising their source and cause. What acting! I sat spellbound. Irving rather scared me – all in black with raven hair and great black ostrich feathers erect in his cap, but with a white face and sorrow possessing him.

And then Ophelia came on. Her beauty caught my breath. Her voice made me want to cry. The other day I came across what Virginia Woolf wrote of Ellen Terry: 'That marvellous voice that stirred the heart-strings to strange emotion. When she spoke it was as if someone drew a bow over a ripe, richly seasoned cello.'[9]

Ellen Terry was very tall and very thin, dressed in white, with a cluster of golden hair – bobbed as we should say nowadays – and every movement was the epitome of grace. Child as I was, I fell head over heels in love with her. No difficulty here about understanding the plot or at least the crux of it. She was hurt by Hamlet's treatment and was so unhappy that she went mad and drowned herself. Oh, the poor, poor thing!

I had a little pocket money and the next day I saw a photo of her as Ophelia in a shop window in Bond Street, Leeds, together with one of Irving. They were marked at one shilling. I went in and bought Ophelia and there it is, a little faded, on my wall in front of me as I write, seventy years later.

Two years after this, in 1881, Irving and Ellen Terry came again to Leeds. I was on fire! Surely the family would go to see them, and surely now that I was nearly fourteen, they would take me with them? But no. What was I to do? I had an uncle who tipped me sovereigns when we stayed with him. I put them in the Penny Savings Bank with the result that I was now a capitalist to the tune of about £3. Rich enough, anyway, to buy four Dress Circle seats at the enhanced prices. So, without

---

[9] This is likely to be a misquotation from Virginia Woolf's essay 'Ellen Terry', published in *The Moment* (London: Hogarth Press, 1947). Woolf, British novelist and essayist (1882-1941), wrote: 'When she spoke it was as if someone drew a bow over a ripe, richly seasoned 'cello; it grated, it glowed, and it growled.' Virginia Woolf, *Collected Essays*, Vol. 4, (London: Hogarth Press, 1967), 67.

2. Alfred Austin in the drawing room at Swinford Old Manor.
   (The Print Collector/Heritage-Images)

saying a word I went into town, secured the seats in the very middle of the front row and returned home.

Everybody was very pleased and Papa, Mama, Aggie and I duly went (at night this time, an added joy!) to see Irving and Ellen Terry in *The Cup* by Tennyson,[10] preceded by a *lever de rideau*, *The Belle's Stratagem*.[11]

No need to tell what it meant to me. What I want to put on record is that the evening established my sister's love of the theatre and there was also an appreciation on the part of my parents which stood me in good stead thereafter.

The Belle's Stratagem was an eighteenth-century farce and there cannot be many who can say they've seen the great Irving of the Lyceum in a farcical comedy. He was inimitably funny and had the house in a roar. As Letitia Hardy, my goddess (Ellen Terry) stood fast on her pedestal for keeps. But I chiefly remember her as Camma in *The Cup*.

In the first act, she sang a little song to a lyre. I have often heard her tell how she managed it and how nervous she was because she had no singing voice. She has had many imitators since – we call them *diseuses* – but she was the first and so attractive was it that she used to be asked to sing it when she was out in society. She always refused: she knew it would lose its effect out of its setting.

For the next five years, school absorbed my energies, but the old passion for the theatre was only dormant. I devoured every book I could get hold of that had to do with the stage. I knew its history from the days of Queen Elizabeth and the lives of the actors and actresses and the parts that had made them famous, from Burbage to Macready.[12] Someone lent me bound volumes of the magazine *Theatre*. I read the lot and learned a great deal.

In 1886, Irving came again to Leeds with *Faust*, but alas without Ellen Terry.[13] Her part as Margaret was taken by her sister Marion.[14] She was very reminiscent of Ellen, had the Terry charm and her pathos was wonderful. It was, indeed, a beautiful performance, but oh, the difference to me. I took her to my heart *faute de mieux* for Ellen's sake, little imagining that we should one day act together and become close friends. The part of Faust was taken by a very handsome young man who was a very gallant lover. His name was George Alexander[15] – my future manager! I was able to appreciate Irving's greatness much more now. He was

---

[10] *The Cup*, by Alfred, Lord Tennyson (first performed at the Lyceum, London, 3 January, 1881).

[11] *The Belle's Stratagem*, by Hannah Cowley, first produced in 1780, 'a comedy centring on shrewd female manipulation (…) a standard repertory piece well into the nineteenth century.' Stuart Curran, *The Cambridge Companion to British Romanticism* (Cambridge: Cambridge University Press, 1993), 183. A *lever de rideau* was a short piece that acted as a curtain-raiser to the main production.

[12] Richard Burbage (c. 1568–1619), English actor and theatre owner. A partner, with Shakespeare, in the Globe Theatre, he played the title role in many of the first performances of the Shakespeare plays, including *Hamlet*, *Othello*, *Richard III* and *King Lear*. William Charles Macready (1793–1873), English actor, manager and diarist, a leading figure in the development of acting and production techniques in the nineteenth century.

[13] This production of *Faust*, adapted by William Gorman Wills from the play by Johann Wolfgang von Goethe, was first staged at the Lyceum in December 1885 after five years of planning. Correspondence between Wills and Irving shows that Irving took great personal interest in the progress of the adaptation and, at various stages, had given his opinion on scenes and characterisations. (Henry Irving Correspondence, The Henry Irving Foundation Centenary Project, www.henryirving.co.uk) 'These protracted and elaborate preparations resulted in probably the most spectacular triumph of his management.' George Rowell, *Theatre in the Age of Irving* (Oxford: Basil Blackwell 1981), 26.

[14] Marion Terry (1852–1930), English actress, younger sister of Ellen Terry. Critic Clement Scott praised her as 'one of the very sweetest English-speaking actresses of her time,' particularly in comedy. *The Drama of Yesterday and Today*, Vol. II, (London: Macmillan, 1899), 324–5.

[15] George Alexander (1858–1918), born George Alexander Gibb Samson, actor-manager who took over the St James's Theatre in 1890 and produced his first play there at the end of January, 1891. Accounts of his management of the St James's Theatre include Barry Duncan, *The St James's Theatre: Its Strange and Complete History, 1835-1957* (London: Barrie and Rockliff, 1964), W. Macqueen-Pope, *St James's, Theatre of Distinction* (London: W. H. Allen, 1958), and A. E. W. Mason, *Sir George Alexander and the St James' Theatre* (London: Macmillan, 1935).

superb as Mephistopheles, conveying in the most extraordinary way that he *was* a spirit – a spirit of evil with immense power.

After I had been ten years at school, my mother insisted I must leave and 'come out'. So, in 1886, at the age of eighteen, I made my debut at a big ball in Leeds. I led this society existence for a year – including a three-week London season under the aegis of Aunt Mary – but no match appeared in the offing and my mother sat me down to speak seriously about my future. If I did not marry, or have a vocation, on my parents' death I would not be left enough to live on; I should have to work to augment it.

Well, I had no vocation and I was determined not to make a 'mixed' marriage. Moreover, I did not want to face life unequipped and too late to do the equipping. My father saw it too. So it was decided I should return to the high school to get the Cambridge Higher Local Certificate with a view to teaching. Meanwhile, we were to 'wait and see'. I was not altogether sorry. I hated the idea of teaching, but the society round also had no fascination for me and I was glad to get into some sort of harness again. September 1886, therefore, saw me back at the Leeds Girls' High School as a pupil teacher (unpaid) in return for tuition.

In the summer holidays the following year, I went on a round of visits in London and I was taken to see Charles Wyndham and Mary Moore in *David Garrick* and also in Sheridan's *The School for Scandal* at the Criterion.[16] Wyndham was a delightful comedian and an actor of great personal charm. My wide reading now stood me in good stead; I could appreciate every point because I knew what to look out for.

Before returning home, I stayed with some cousins in Richmond and they were good enough to take me to see the Kendals in *Lady Clancarty* at the St James's Theatre.[17] Suffice to say that Ellen Terry had spoilt me for Mrs Madge Kendal; I thought her artificial and I never changed my mind, though later I came to realise she was a great artiste. She was a past mistress of technique, but she always left me cold. Little did I dream, as I watched Mrs Kendal that day, that I would tread the boards of the St James's myself or that she would one day accept and produce a play of mine!

At the end of three years, I passed my exams with honours, but as I richly deserved, *second class* – for the very good reason that I had spent far too much time founding the Leeds Girls' High School Drama Society and producing five plays!

Once that society had been launched, there had arisen the question of some sort of scenery. We had a large gymnasium with a small platform, that was all. So, as usual, I took the plunge: I wrote a letter addressed to 'The Head Carpenter, Grand Theatre, Leeds'. The result was an interview and, for the first time in my life, I

---

[16] Charles Wyndham (1837–1919) and Mary Moore (1861–1931), partners in the management of the Criterion and Wyndham's Theatres. They married in 1916. The Criterion Theatre in Piccadilly opened in 1874, and was reconstructed in 1884. Wyndham's, still a working theatre on Charing Cross Road, was opened on 16 November 1899: Allardyce Nicoll, *A History of English Drama, 1660-1900*, Vol. V, *Late Nineteenth Century Drama, 1850-1900* (Cambridge: Cambridge University Press, 1959), 222. *David Garrick* by Thomas William Robertson. This comedy, in three acts, had its premiere at the Prince of Wales Theatre in Birmingham in April 1864 and was successful enough to move to the Haymarket in London later that month. Edward Sothern was originally in the title role later made famous by Charles Wyndham. *The School for Scandal* by Richard Brinsley Sheridan was first performed at the Drury Lane Theatre in May, 1777. It became among the most celebrated comedies of manners, exposing the follies and vices of the age. It was often cited by Victorian theatre managers and critics as a representative 'legitimate' comedy of the old English school.

[17] *Lady Clancarty; or, Wedded and Wooed* by Tom Taylor (first performed 9 March, 1874 at the Olympic Theatre). The acting partnership of Madge Kendal (1849–1935) and her husband, William Hunter Kendal (1843–1917). The main source of information about the Kendals comes from Madge Kendal's autobiographical writings, *Dame Madge Kendal, by Herself* (London: John Murray, 1933), and *Dramatic Opinions* (Boston: Little, Brown, and Company, 1890).

entered a theatre by the stage door. Mr Charker was an oldish man with a walrus moustache and within ten minutes or so we were sworn friends. I think he was immensely tickled by my boldness – there was such a twinkle in his eye.

'Would tha like to come oop on't stage?' he said. Wouldn't I! It was a shock. The night before I had sat in the Dress Circle to see *Sweet Lavender* performed by a touring company.[18] Now the whole stage area was draped in dust sheets and the effect was ghostly. In the middle of the huge stage, a small scene with a writing table had been set. I sat down and wrote my name on the blotter: Winifred Dolan. I wonder what Lavender made of it that night? Having settled details and come to terms with Mr Charker, I walked back into the real world – again through the stage door, feeling very professional.

Those school performances were attended by the press and we had the advantage of criticism. It is true the critics were very good, especially to me. I learned a lot and gained something of a local reputation. This brought me the offer to play the lead in a charity show which proved the turning point in my life. But something wonderful befell me before that and here is the place to tell of it.

While we were waiting to know whether I had passed the final exam, I went on a visit to my uncle Alfred Austin's home in Kent – a lovely Jacobean house called Swinford Old Manor. A visit there was one of the greatest pleasures in life. It was the high summer of 1890 and the weather was glorious.

One morning at breakfast, my Aunt Hester was opening her letters when she said to her husband: 'Irving and Ellen Terry are staying at Deal, they want to come over for the day. How about Wednesday …?' My heart missed a beat. Could it be really true? Was I going to meet Ellen Terry and Irving too, hear them talk, actually *know* them? What luck, for I was there until Saturday. And then, just before the selected day, another letter came: a problem had arisen and 'might they come next week instead'? Next week – when I should be gone!

Young people have a capacity for suffering under disappointment that is seldom realised by their elders who expect them to be reasonable. It took me all my society manners to carry the blow. But there was another guest staying in the house, Mrs Ashley Dodd, who was also leaving on the Saturday. Mrs A.D. made no bones about *her* disappointment until at last Aunt Hester very politely invited her to stay on, adding 'and Win, you can stay too if you like'. Bless her warm Irish heart! She *knew*. Was there not a tell-tale row of Ellen Terry photographs set out on the chest of drawers in my bedroom upstairs? They must have spoken for me!

The day arrived at last and they came. My uncle and aunt met them at the door. Mrs Ashley Dodd and I waited in the drawing room and through the open door I heard that marvellous voice say, 'Oh, you have company,' and Aunt Hester's reassuring reply:

'No, no, only a friend and a little niece of mine who are staying with us.'

Now it is not etiquette to invite people to meet great public characters; it is they who are asked to consent to meet private folk – quite another thing! I suddenly understood why Aunt Hester had been so icily polite when her guest had forced her hand. Only those who dwell habitually in the public eye can know the value they set on privacy in their personal contacts.

The next moment they were in the room – Irving very tall and rather grim, squiring the lady. She – how different, impossible to describe! The impact of her

---

[18] *Sweet Lavender* by Arthur Wing Pinero – 'a domestic drama in three acts' – had its premiere at Terry's Theatre in London on 21 March 1888. It ran for 684 performances and subsequently enjoyed numerous revivals.

personality was overpowering; without the slightest conscious effort, she filled the room with a blaze of warmth and light – 'all gay, all dancing stars'. And lest you should think this the natural hyperbole of a silly stage-struck girl of 22, read this poem by Vita Sackville-West about Ellen Terry.[19] And remember, she had not seen her in her prime, only in the sunset of her days: but I had seen her in 1879!

A memory to me, I young; she old
A player dies and all her art with her
As with the winter dies the marigold
But oh my heart! Could ever I transfer
To paper as her last interpreter
Such worship as I then to her bespoke
In those green years, those callow generous times,

Then would Shakespeare clot into one line
Ellen! Too human to be called divine.

She was all woman to me, all the rhymes
Hung by the young Orlando on the oak
She was all leaves, all gay, all dancing stars
All solemn cellos and all light guitars

Ellen, beyond the Paradisal bars
Do you and Shakespeare meet and weep and joke?

Of course, she was older now and no longer thin; she was 43, a beautiful woman in her glorious prime. It had nothing to do with glamour. Glamour is the necessary stock-in-trade of all actresses who become idols of the public (who little know the woman behind the façade). There was an integrity of character and disposition – today we look for 'sex appeal', but Ellen Terry appealed straight to the human heart. Have you noticed how the poetess echoes Virginia Woolf's comparison of that inimitable voice to a cello?

They had brought a girl with them – a Miss Audrey Campbell. Of course I was told to entertain her, 'show her the garden that I loved'[20] and so on. I wished her at Jericho! Uncle Alfred carried off Irving while Aunt Hester and Mrs Ashley Dodd had Ellen Terry more or less to themselves. She did find time to spare me a word or two, though I confess I can't remember a syllable – I was too overcome. After luncheon, Miss Campbell took a photograph of us in the garden. She sent me a copy afterwards but it was so badly 'fixed' that it quickly faded away. What a treasure it would have been today!

Two days later I was home again. Then, in December came that offer to play the lead in a charity show. The play was *New Men And Old Acres*, stage-managed by a clever amateur from Bradford named C.V. France.[21] (He went on the stage

---

[19] Victoria ('Vita') Sackville-West (1892–1962), English novelist and poet. This poem was probably written around 1928 at the time of Ellen Terry's death. In this period, Sackville-West came to know Edith (Edy) Craig (Terry's daughter) and her partner Christopher St John (Christabel Marshall).

[20] Her choice of words here is a reference to Alfred Austin's only truly popular book, *The Garden that I Love* (London: Macmillan, 1894). It was a work in prose of a type known as 'garden diaries', which relished the charm of Swinford Old Manor.

[21] *New Men and Old Acres*, a comedy in three acts by Tom Taylor and Augustus W. Dubourg. Winifred Dolan's role was Lilian Vavasour, a part played by Mrs Kendal when it was first performed at the Haymarket in London in October 1869, and later reprised by Ellen Terry. C.V. France (1868–1949), English stage actor, later in films, including *A Yank at Oxford* (1938) and *Night Train To Munich* (1940).

himself shortly afterwards and made a name in 'old man' parts.) The play was a great success and I had a very gratifying reception.

The next day was a Saturday. I was sitting with my mother talking it over when she said: 'Two men asked to be introduced to me – one was the manager at The Grand and he said his friend was also a manager somewhere. They wished to congratulate me on my daughter's performance. One of them said: "I suppose, of course, she will adopt the stage as a profession?" But I said "certainly not," and they bowed themselves off.' (I could see them with their tails between their legs, poor things!)

A moment's dead silence, and then under my breath I said, half to myself, 'I wish to God I could!'

To my astonishment, my mother said: 'Do you want to go on the stage?'

'More than anything in the world,' I replied, 'only I suppose as a Catholic ...'

'What has that got to do with it?' she said, 'there are lots of Catholics on the stage: Kate and Mary Rorke, for instance.[22] And what about Mrs Siddons and all the Kembles?'[23]

'But I thought ...'

'My dear child, you can serve God and save your soul in any walk of life. Don't be a prig. It all depends on yourself.'

Quickly I said: 'Would you let me go?'

'Oh well, I must talk that over with your father. There's a lot to ...'

'I'll go and talk to my father now,' I said, and went into the next room where he was smoking and reading *The Tablet*[24] before the fire.

'Papa! Will you allow me to go on the stage?' He laid down his paper, took his pipe out of his mouth and looked at me.

'I am told you have real talent. You have shown a strong character at school and we can trust you. So, if you want it, the answer is yes.' And with that he put his pipe back in his mouth and resumed his paper.

I was astounded. I couldn't take it in. I went back to my mother. 'He said yes!!'

It was as simple as that.

---

[22] Mary Rorke (1858–1938), English actress, and her sister Kate (1866–1945). Kate Rorke worked with actor-managers John Hare, Herbert Beerbohm-Tree, and George Alexander. Donald Mullin, *Victorian Actors and Actresses in Review* (Westport, Conn.: Greenwood Press, 1983) 393. Clement Scott called her 'One of the best of our young English actresses of what I call the Mrs Kendal school, human, tender, and true,' *The Drama of Yesterday and Today*, Vol. II, (London: Macmillan, 1899), 329.

[23] Sarah Siddons (1755–1831), English actress, the best-known tragedienne of the eighteenth century. Her father, Roger Kemble, was an actor-manager, and she had eleven siblings, seven of whom went on the stage. Sarah Siddons was the great-great grand niece of John Kemble (1599–1679), who was beatified and canonised as a Roman Catholic saint in the twentieth century.

[24] British Catholic weekly newspaper.

Chapter II

'Why, then the world's mine oyster'
– The Merry Wives of Windsor

That night, I sat down and wrote to Clement Scott, the drama critic of the *Daily Telegraph*.[1] I know now that he was the doyen of all the London critics, occupying a position similar to that of the famous Francisque Sarcey of *Le Figaro* in Paris.[2] I can't remember exactly what I wrote except that, greatly daring, I asked him to tell me how a provincial girl with no influence who desired to go on the stage should set about it. This is the letter I received by return of post:

> 52, Lincoln's Inn Fields,
> London, WC
> 22 December 1890

Dear Miss Dolan,

I don't mind confessing that your kind letter has interested me very deeply. The proof of it is that I am sitting down to answer it overwhelmed as I am with Christmas work and responsibilities. You don't know what the life of a drama critic is like at Christmas time.

I must tell you I receive countless letters of the same pattern. No, not of the same pattern, for they come for the most part from the frivolous, the empty-headed and the vain. Your letter is that of an earnest, enthusiastic, educated girl. The others mean vanity whereas you mean work.

And then you are a Catholic and that brings me nearer to you, for there we are brother and sister or father and child as you will.

There is so much to be said on the subject, so much I would like to say. The path is so dangerous, do beware of it. The ascent is so steep and it would break your young enthusiastic heart. What am I to do? I want to talk to you, but I am going to the South of France and shall not be back in England until the end of January – but still I want to help you.

Let me see you when it is possible on my return to London and write me one line before I leave England next Saturday. I will interest Irving and Ellen Terry on your behalf, be sure.

Yours sincerely,
Clement Scott

---

[1] Clement Scott (1841–1904), outspoken drama critic of the *Daily Telegraph* from 1871. Also playwright, travel writer and founder and editor of the magazine *Theatre*.
[2] Francisque Sarcey (1827–1899), French journalist and drama critic, a regular contributor to *Le Figaro*, *L'Illustration*, *Le Gaulois*, *Le XIX' Siècle*, *L'Opinion nationale*, and *Le Temps*.

Imagine receiving a letter like that! Now please bear in mind this was still the Victorian era – no girl could go about unchaperoned. How was I to go to London and call upon a man? A friend I had met during my year in society came to my rescue. Mrs Murray Hickson[3] was a young widow who lived at Esher in Surrey when she was not keeping house for her father, a County Court judge, when his official duties brought him to Leeds. She invited me to stay with her and offered to accompany me to the decisive interview.

In due course, I went to Esher, a date was fixed and we travelled to London to see the great man. He was a perfect dear! He began by repeating much of what he had said in his letter and spent half an hour trying to discourage me: the difficulties were enormous; the moral dangers not to be lightly discarded; the profession a closed corporation; influence of paramount importance; stage life a gamble – plenty of room at the top but, between the rungs of the ladder, at best heartbreak, at worst despair.

Mr Scott said that people who caught the stage fever were so besotted they would never quit however unsuccessful – they sank and sank but hung on grimly even at the cost of semi-starvation and wasted lives. I listened and when he had finished I said: 'I think I know all that. I have faced it. I only want my chance to make good. If I fail, I will accept the verdict and I shall quit. Please give me my chance.'

I shall never forget his smile. He had been trying me out. He said briskly: 'Very well. Now you mean business. All the old stagers learned their job in two great stock companies …'

'Bath and Bristol'! I interjected.

He laughed appreciatively and went on: 'They are gone. There is only one left – at Margate in Kent. Miss Sarah Thorne takes pupils for a fee.[4] Go to her for six months and then come and see me again. Good luck and God bless you.'

My mother and I later went to fix things up with Miss Thorne, who lived somewhere in West Kensington. She was a dear lady – most respectable. She quite dispelled the qualms of my mother who, I think, had begun to have misgivings at the way her duckling was taking to water.

The interview was not without its humour. My mother said: 'I should never allow my daughter to wear tights.'

But Miss T was equal to the occasion: 'My young ladies never wear tights,' she said. 'I train for the legitimate.'[5]

---

[3] Probably Mabel Murray Hickson (1859–1922), who later had some modest success as a writer of short fiction and poetry, including two collections of stories, *A Latter-Day Romance* (Publisher unknown, 1893) and *Concerning Teddy* (London: J. Bowden, 1897). After her second marriage, she wrote under the delightful name of Mabel Greenhow Kitkat.

[4] Sarah Thorne (1836–1899), doyenne of repertory theatre in England at that time. She succeeded her father as lessee of the Theatre Royal, Margate in 1867 with her declared aim 'to offer the newest pieces approved in the metropolis as occasion permits but never to neglect old and legitimate productions'. (*Era*, 4 August 1867). She ran the theatre until 1873 when it was sold. Her second period there began in 1879, and she opened what is generally regarded as the country's first formal drama school in 1885.

[5] The bestowal of Letters Patent by Charles II on Thomas Killigrew and William Davenant after Charles' restoration to the throne in 1660 reserved to their theatres in London (Drury Lane and Covent Garden) and others with the Royal imprimatur throughout Britain, the monopoly rights to perform the spoken drama in Britain. These were known as the 'Patent theatres' and generally designated 'Theatre Royal' (for example, Theatre Royal at Margate at which Dolan makes her debut). The monopoly rights of the Patent theatres to perform the spoken drama were enforced by the Theatres Act of 1737, and were debated in the 1832 House of Commons Select Committee on Dramatic Literature. The rights of the Patent houses were not removed until the 1843 Theatres Regulation Act, while censorship of scripts by the Lord Chamberlain's office remained until 1968. The 'spoken drama' or 'regular drama' was also known as the 'legitimate drama', as it represented an amalgam of law and customary practice in the theatre industry. After 1843, the 'legitimate' drama became less a legal term and more indicative of aesthetic valuations of some genres – particularly verse tragedy and high comedy – over illegitimate entertainments such as melodrama, burlesque, pantomime, puppet theatre and musicals, all of which relied on song, dance, and spectacle, rather than words. Dolan's memoir demonstrates that outdated legal categories of drama still carried social and aesthetic value.

3. The redoubtable Sarah Thorne. **(Sarah Thorne Theatre Club)**

It was Greek to my mother, but the wise lady had guessed that she had been thinking of burlesque and panto. The fee was £26 and it was agreed I should join the company at Margate on 1 May 1891 when her season opened. Two more months to wait!

We went home again for me to take my leave of our friends. They were all thrilled when they heard I was going on the stage and gave me a wonderful send-off. The school and staff presented me with a silver-mounted dressing bag and the committee a cheque for £15. Other presents included a cabin trunk ('for when you go to America'), a travelling flask, opera glasses and a handsome umbrella (in memory of *Rosabella!*).

An old lady whom I had dearly loved had left me £100 when she died so, on 30 April 1891, with this capital, all my belongings and high hopes, my father put me on the train at Leeds. I was launched into the world to sink or swim.

The old Theatre Royal at Margate had one of the richest histories of any theatre in the country. It was the last of the old 'patent' theatres, ranking in that respect with the Theatres Royal of Bath, Bristol and York. In its time it had seen the triumphs of such famous players as Edmund Kean, Mrs Siddons and Charles Mathews. It was the last real 'stock' theatre in the country and Miss Thorne was a member of a well-known theatrical family.

Upon my arrival, I drove in a cab to her house and asked if I might leave my trunk there while I went to look for lodgings. 'My dear child,' she cried, 'do you mean to say you have come *alone*? I will give you an address. Go and see Mrs Blair, she lives just opposite the stage door. If she can take you in, she will look after you very well.'

I went. And she did. She was a plump, motherly lady with a pretty daughter. I had a small bedroom and a tiny sitting room about 10 feet square and she fed me like a turkey cock – all for £2 a week. It was my first experience of theatrical landladies, who are a race apart. They will nurse you when you are ill, darn your socks if you are a man and keep you in order if you are inclined to be flighty. 'Gentlemen are *not* to be invited home to supper!' God bless those landladies. The touring actors and actresses are ever ready to acknowledge the debt they owe them. Next day there was a rehearsal call for 10am and Miss Thorne introduced all the newcomers to each other and to a few old-timers from last year's season. There were about twenty of us. Then, parts were handed out to some of us and I was one of the lucky ones. The script consisted merely of cues and lines, but I could see it was an *ingénue* role with plenty of comedy in it. I had to pick up the play as we went along. The bill posters, already up, announced the play as *The World Against Her*.[6] It was in five acts and I forget how many scenes – obviously a melodrama.

We started rehearsals at once. The leading lady, on the strength of being last season's pupil, gave herself tremendous airs. It was she who had 'the world against her', was kidnapped and imprisoned until rescued by the leading man. The villain was played by Lyall Swete and he really bore the play on his shoulders.[7] Then there was Bee Berkeley, a tall girl with a face rather like a handsome horse. She was as good as gold in this one, but really her line was wicked women.

Now, in 1891, no *lady* ever crossed her legs, she crossed her ankles instead. So, if you crossed your legs and showed five inches of shin, especially if, in so doing, you revealed a seductive rose-pink frilly petticoat, the audience knew at once what to expect. But if you added a cigarette, you were beyond the pale, past redemption, a villainess in excelsis! Bee was all that. Heroines, on the other hand, were expected to be virtuous to the point of inanity, while the most popular 'stock' hero was the gentleman-roué who always made good in the final act.

To this day I remember with glee in some melodrama or other the audible shudder that ran through the pit when the hero of this type came into the public house and lit his cigar with a £5 note! Yes, audiences were very unsophisticated in those days – they would weep and laugh and hiss the villain … and thoroughly enjoy themselves.

To return to my debut at the Theatre Royal. There was an extraordinarily large man in the company who supplied the low comedy while my 'lover' and I were responsible for the light comedy. My lover! He (who shall be nameless) was a man of about forty with brown hair, but prematurely bald and much shorter than myself. It seemed he wanted to be a playwright and had come to learn something of stage technique. He had never acted in his life!

After we were pat with our words, we had a band rehearsal for music cues. The orchestra was a family affair – their name was Gates. Mrs Gates played the piano, or harmonium in 'church' scenes, Percy the violin, Alf the cornet, while Harold (in knickerbockers) worked the side-drum. Pa Gates sat with a double-bass between his knees and drew the bow across to emit a deep 'plom-plom' in tense moments which, happily, were rare. He did not add much to the ensemble, but it looked well. The conductor was a Miss Ballard.

At last the sun rose on 17 May 1891. It was Whit Monday and we were told to expect a bumper house for the bank holiday. As we sat making up in the dressing rooms that night, we could hear through the thin walls the audience assembling. We

---

[6] *The World Against Her,* by Frank Harvey (circa 1887). Little is known about this melodrama, except that it had a very short run at Her Majesty's in 1895. Nicoll gives a list of performances in Preston (January 1887), the Grand, Islington (August 1887) and the Surrey (July 1888). The play was hugely successful in Melbourne, Australia in 1888 and revived in Hobart in 1903. The posters for this latter production summed it up as 'an intensely interesting stage story dealing with the great social question, Is marriage a failure?' (State Library of Tasmania archive.)

[7] Edward Lyall Swete (1865–1930), a noted Shakespearean actor, and a playwright and director, who frequently worked in New York.

were on the same storey as the gallery and to judge by the nut-cracking, whistling and amiable back-chat, we were in for a lively time.

And so it proved. Mr Wade, one of the old-timers, was my 'father' and we made our first entrance together. I was never so nervous in my life – just a cloth behind me and not so much as a chair to keep me company. Mr Wade whispered: 'Give it to 'em hot. There's our cue. Come on!' And then we were on and the ice was broken.

Next came a scene with my lover; it didn't go too badly but he mumbled with fright and as he had covered his bald pate with a reddish wig, they kept shouting 'Speak up, ginger!' And when we came to the love scene in which he proposes and I accept him, the poor man went to pieces altogether. I could see exactly what had happened: he had, as we say, 'stepped out of his part' and found himself, to his embarrassment, making love to *Miss Dolan* in front of all these people! He forgot I was … whatever my name was in the play. Of course he dried hopelessly.

Now the audience that night consisted of townsfolk, with fisher lads in the gallery. They knew the play by heart and actually started prompting him, making matters worse. The last line I had spoken before the hiatus was 'Kiss me, Herbert!' (it was that which had so upset him because we leave out kisses at rehearsal), so I hurled myself into the breach and clasped him in my arms repeating 'Kiss me again, Herbert, kiss me again' *ad nauseam* until the house was convulsed and thundered its applause. We actually got a special call in front of the curtain when it was all over.

Another night when we were playing this piece, there was a second *contre-temps.* I had a little scene on the stage by myself this time and my last line should have brought on another character in the cast, but the girl was missing and there was a 'stage wait'. I improvised for about three minutes (an agonisingly long time in a play). The next entrance after the missing girl's was the leading lady's and *she* wouldn't come on for fear the audience would think she was to blame for the wait. Dear Miss Thorne came to the rescue, literally shoving her out on to the stage.

I am ashamed to confess that I was rather disgusted at being cast in such stuff as this full-blooded melodrama. But it taught me a lesson: I realised after that first night the value of broad effects (so essential when playing in large theatres, especially in the provinces). Also, nowadays the ham actor is taboo but I have often thought how useful such training is and would be to the modern naturalistic actor when he had to tackle Lear or Mark Antony's speech in *Julius Caesar*, for instance. Miss Thorne knew her job.

The bill changed twice a week and we were rehearsed in the classics, farce, domestic drama and drawing-room comedy. Shakespeare and Sheridan were not attempted until circumstances permitted, that is to say when some former pupil who had made good in a small way in London came down for a week or two for further practice, when they would be given star billing.

We were expected to attend all rehearsals, sitting in front if not personally engaged in the piece being rehearsed. We might be required to 'walk on' in crowds or as guests. One learned valuable experience in 'dressing the stage', by-play and so forth. There was also a fencing class which I attended. We were kept pretty busy and I was perfectly happy.

We had our little sensations, too. One recruit was a Bensonian[8] who always

---

[8] Any actor who'd learned his craft under the great Shakespearean actor-manager, Frank Benson (1858–1939).

wore plus-fours; he soon got engaged to Miss Blakiston – an idyll which was no sooner on than off. Then there were two flashy girls who called themselves Montmorency; one was brunette, the other blonde. One day, Mr Wade and the blonde went to London and returned in time for the evening show – married. Unfortunately, the girl turned out to be a Ward in Chancery and there were legal proceedings.[9] Miss Thorne was furious.

Another day the ladies in the company were all agog because a new man was coming 'who had been an attaché somewhere'. He turned out to be very handsome and aristocratic, but he didn't stay long: he was no more promising as an actor than he had apparently been as a diplomat.

But at last a greater sensation caused a real flutter in the dove-cote. Ellen Terry's son, Gordon Craig, known as 'Teddy', who was playing small parts at the Lyceum, came to join us for a short time.[10] Miss Thorne was going to put on Sheridan Knowles' blank verse drama, *The Hunchback,* for him and she cast me to play opposite him, Teddy acting Modus and I Helen (one of his mother's parts long before she met Irving).[11]

This was my first costume – or period – play and I had to study manner. I was, of course, elated, but very, very nervous for here my past experience as an amateur stood me in no stead at all. Teddy Craig was delightful to act with, but Miss Thorne gave me no help whatever. She left me to see what I could make of it.

After we had played *The Hunchback* some half a dozen times, she was on the stage one day at rehearsal and, coming behind me, put her fingers under my elbows and lifted my arms. 'Never make a gesture with a bent arm, dear, always from the shoulder,' she said. It was the first criticism she had yet passed on me.

'Oh, Miss Thorne,' I said, 'do tell me. Am I any good?'

'My dear,' she replied, 'I can teach you nothing. It is all there. What you want is practice – try to play as many parts as you can possibly get hold of. You are the legitimate successor of Maude Millet!'[12]

I could have kissed her.

Another recruit joined us about this time, a very charming boy whose name was Granville Barker,[13] destined to become a household name as a producer. Miss Thorne put up *Hamlet* for Teddy Craig and he gave a very scholarly performance in the title part, though immature of course. He was to make his name not as an actor, but as a stage designer on revolutionary lines. He was never a prophet in his own country, but Russia, Germany and Italy welcomed him with open arms.

Next, Miss Evelyn Millard joined us for a time and became our leading lady.[14] She played Juliet in *Romeo and Juliet* very, very charmingly. She was

---

[9] A minor who was under legal guardianship.

[10] Edward Gordon Craig, (1872–1966), English actor and designer. After he tired of acting, Craig became an innovative and successful stage designer in Europe. Biographies include *Edward Gordon Craig* by Denis Bablet (London: Heinemann, 1966) and *Gordon Craig – The Story of His Life* by Edward Craig (London: Alfred A Knopf, 1968).

[11] *The Hunchback*, by the Irish dramatist, James Sheridan Knowles, was first produced at Covent Garden in 1832, with the part of Julia specially written for Fanny Kemble (1809–1893). Mullin, *Victorian Plays*, gives a substantial list of its many revivals over the nineteenth century, 158–9.

[12] Maude Millet (1867–1920), much-photographed English actress, particularly successful in *ingénue* and light comedy roles.

[13] Harley Granville Barker (1877–1946), English actor and later a successful producer and director. He was, indeed, a boy when he joined Miss Thorne's Margate company, being not yet 14. See Dennis Kennedy, *Granville Barker and the Dream of the Theatre* (Cambridge: Cambridge University Press, 1985).

[14] Evelyn Millard (1869–1941), English actress, who made her first appearance in a walk-on at the Haymarket, before arriving at Margate. Her Juliet for Miss Thorne was the start of a successful career playing Shakespearean heroines for various companies, including her own, which she formed in 1908.

sweetly pretty and her diction was perfect – her father was a well-known teacher of elocution in London. She was to make her name one day as Flavia in *The Prisoner of Zenda* at the St James's Theatre.[15]

In mid-season, Miss Thorne took her annual benefit – an old custom, now obsolete.[16] It was a great occasion. Actors and actresses who had graduated under her guidance and were now veterans on the London stage came to support her, each contributing something to the programme. Among them was Charles Rock, and I was chosen to play the title role with him in *The Pretty Horsebreaker*, a lovely comedy part.[17] In front of the curtain during one of the intervals, Granville Barker's mother gave a wonderful exhibition of bird calls and to crown the evening, dear old Miss Thorne herself gave a short scene from *Much Ado* as Beatrice. It was rather painful, but very touching.

Soon after that, we were told we were going on tour. 'Where?' we asked, and were told 'on the Kentish circuit'. It sounded portentous but, *entre nous*, it was really what was called a 'fit-up tour', i.e. playing the public halls and corn exchanges in places that had no local theatre. Sometimes we played a week, but more often three-night stands. The 'Kent circuit' also included places in Surrey such as Leatherhead, Dorking, Guildford and Kingston.

I shared digs with Bee Berkeley and, of course, Teddy Craig came on tour with us. It was a most amusing experience and we had such fine weather that summer of 1891. At Leatherhead, Miss Thorne gave the company a treat – a day's picnic to Box Hill in wagonettes.[18]

But it's Canterbury that's written on my heart for it was there that Irving and Ellen Terry came down to see Teddy and me. Another ordeal to go through! We played the Mordus and Helen scenes and then I was out of the bill again until I played in *The World Against Her*. Thus I had a day and a night free, so Uncle Alfred invited me to spend it at Swinford, as Irving and Ellen Terry were coming to luncheon again. Off I went, careful to take my precious photographs with me lest they should be stolen from my lodgings while I was away. It was lucky indeed I did.

When Irving and Ellen Terry drove up to the door where we were gathered to greet them, Ellen cried out: 'Why there she is! My dear child, Henry and I drove up to your lodgings to pick you up and they said you were out.' To this day it is a source of bitter regret that I did not have that drive.

This time there was no Mrs Ashley Dodd and no Miss Audrey Campbell, so Aunt Hester asked me to take Ellen Terry upstairs to remove her hat. I took her to my room. She looked at my photographs, then looked at me and said: 'What does your mother say about your going on the stage?'

'Oh,' I said, 'she is quite pleased, but of course I wouldn't have gone against my parents' wishes.'

---

[15] *The Prisoner of Zenda* by Edward E. Rose (first performed at the St James's, January 1896), adapted from the novel by Anthony Hope.
[16] The benefit system was a way of supplementing the salaries of members of the acting company, and was often included in contract negotiations. A benefit was an especially arranged performance, with a proportion of the box office takings going to the named recipient of the benefit. The benefit performance would generally feature the benefit recipient in favourite roles. Tickets were usually sold at a premium, and their purchase was a way of indicating patronage and favour.
[17] Charles Rock (1866–1919), English actor who accompanied John Hare on his first American tour in 1895. Between 1912 and 1919, he appeared in nearly 50 silent films. *The Pretty Horsebreaker* by William Brough and Andrew Halliday (1861).
[18] Light, four-wheeled, horse-drawn carriages designed to carry a large number of passengers sitting on long bench-style seats facing each other.

The next moment she was hugging me hard. 'That's all right, then. Come along – and bring those photographs down with you.'

This time it was like a family party. Even Irving unbent. After luncheon, Ellen Terry began signing the photographs: 'Your affectionate friend, Ellen Terry'. Among them was also one of Irving in private life and another of the two of them as Dr Primrose and Olivia in *The Vicar of Wakefield*.[19] She forged Irving's signature (very cleverly too!) on the first and then handed the other over to him, saying: 'Now Henry, you sign this one,' which he did and then she added her own signature to his. Wasn't I proud!

Then Irving took both my hands, drew me towards him and, speaking very gravely, said: 'So you are one of us now?'

'Yes, sir.'

'Remember always to uphold the honour of the Profession.'

'Indeed yes, sir.'

'And in acting remember that thought precedes speech. For instance, do not say "look"! and *then* point, but point *first* and then say "look"! Every sentence expresses a new thought: you must pass the words through your mind before you utter them. It is a question of quick thinking.'

'Thank you, sir,' I replied.

'God bless you my dear,' he said.

It was a wonderful moment, this great actor's lesson to a tyro. I never forgot it.

I went back with them – in the train this time, as Irving was changing at Ashford Junction to return to London. As he got out, I heard him say to Ellen Terry: 'Don't let that child pay her fare' (for I had been bundled in with them, ticketless, by an excited stationmaster). That touch was typical of Irving and the reason we all loved him in the profession. From that day on, I was admitted into Ellen Terry's family circle. Gone was the callow adoration of the past and in its place a close and dear friendship.

After she had seen me play in *The World Against Her,* she sent me this note. It was addressed to 'Mith Dolan', the reason for which will soon become clear:

> My dear ———— ,
>
> Give me a name for you for 'Winnie' has unpleasant associations with an unpleasant person – and unpleasant and you are miles asunder.
>
> I earnestly advise you to make modern comedy your study and to that end the first thing you must learn to do is to stand up as straight as an arrow – think of it every minute of the day and then you will have no need to think of such a trifle at night when you are acting – and so will avoid an appearance of self-consciousness.
>
> You ought to study fencing too at once – it would give you grace with your arms. At present you are somewhat angular, but from this moment pay attention to standing up straight. So much depends on

---

[19] Oliver Goldsmith's novel, *The Vicar of Wakefield* (1766) was adapted many times over the nineteenth century, including J.S. Coyne (1850), although Dolan is more likely to be referring to Irving's 1885 revival of *Olivia*, W.G. Will's adaptation of *The Vicar of Wakefield*. Irving played Dr Primrose (the Vicar), and Terry played the title role. According to Jeffrey Richards, Henry Irving's most recent biographer, the play remained a favourite in the Lyceum repertoire until almost the end of Irving's career. *Sir Henry Irving: A Victorian Actor and his World* (London: Hambledon and London, 2005), 156.

that – voice, beauty etc. I must tell you, dear, your lisp is very strong and would interfere fatally with anything but modern comedy; for that it would not be a drawback.

To be quite frank with your uncle's niece and your most sunny, good, pleasant little self, I consider that if you wish to make a living on the stage, every moment you study anything but modern drama you throw away that moment. If you could get one engagement either in London or 'on tour', say one of Mr Jones's plays or one of Mr Pinero's,[20] it would be the best happening for you and if you will send to me I will recommend you strongly.

Your advantages of up-bringing, your ease, your education, your height, your way of wearing your modern clothes, your natural voice – all these are in your favour and there is no reason whatever why, in a few years' time, you should not be making from £8–10 a week in some good theatres.

I advise you whilst being amiable with most good folk in a theatre, to make your friends outside a theatre. There are only a few exceptional persons in a theatre – at present, at all events – the rest are a rather thriftless, ignorant, good-natured, fratterheaded lot and will scarcely improve you in your part as a brilliant comedy actress.
You ought to go and see all the plays at Mr Hare's theatre and the St James's Theatre and Terry's Theatre.

> With love,
>> Yours always,
>>> Ellen Terry

What a letter from the greatest English actress of the day! And with what tender courtesy she criticised! Do you wonder why people idolised Ellen Terry?

When we were playing at Kingston, I received a truly wonderful surprise. I got a letter from my Uncle Alfred enclosing one from George Alexander, the actor-manager at the St James's Theatre in London. He offered to take me on his staff as an understudy at a guinea a week so that I might get an idea of a London theatre. 'If I find her intelligent, I would try to give her a small part later on.'

Now my six months at Margate were not up until 1 November. Would Miss Thorne let me go? What a greenhorn I was – I did not realise this was a feather in her cap as well as in mine. Of course she was delighted, elated. I was to go *at once*. So I telegraphed 'yes' to my uncle and to Mr Alexander that I was on my way, wrote the news to my mother, packed my cabin trunk and was in London early next morning, presenting myself at the stage door of the St James's Theatre about midday. My foot was on the first rung of Mr Clement Scott's ladder.

---

[20] Henry Arthur Jones (1851–1929) and Arthur Wing Pinero (1855–1934), were prominent playwrights and critics of the late nineteenth century, writing and proselytising for the 'New Drama,' aiming to reform the British theatre, particularly to raise its literary standards.

Chapter III

'O wonderful, wonderful, and most wonderful'
– As You Like It

I want to give you some idea of what London was like when I joined the St James's company in what's been called the 'Naughty Nineties'. We were in the last throes of an era that was passing away to vanish forever in the First World War, although the cloven hoof was not yet showing.

Queen Victoria was still on the throne, Society was Society with a capital S; divorcees were socially outcast and could not be presented at court; ladies did not smoke; entertaining was carried out in the great houses, not in public restaurants; there were no night-clubs or cabarets. Good breeding consisted of strictly avoiding all taboos: for instance, you didn't appear in Rotten Row unless you were dressed to the nines or go shopping in Bond Street after four in the afternoon.[1]

Lillie Langtry was all the rage as a great professional beauty and the Prince of Wales's reigning favourite.[2] People used to stand on chairs in Hyde Park to see her drive past as though she were a peep show. Actors and actresses were not recognised socially unless (as was beginning to be the case) they were people already of social standing who had gone on the stage like Lady Monckton and the Vanbrugh sisters.[3] Legally, we were still 'rogues and vagabonds' (Irving got the act repealed).[4] The great exceptions were Bernhardt (when she played in London), Irving and Ellen Terry.

The Kendals occupied a unique position; they were greatly admired for their propriety: '*so* nice to see love scenes played by husband and wife'. Mrs Kendal was appointed by Princess Mary to be 'reader' to her daughter, the Princess May of Teck, who was engaged to Prince Eddie and would one day be Queen (but not as Eddie's wife. He died and she married his brother, George V).[5]

The carriages of the nobility were great barouches[6] set on C-springs, picked out in red or yellow with a coat of arms on the door panels and two powdered footmen standing on a platform behind. Halfway through this decade, a change set

---

[1] Rotten Row is a broad sandy track running along the south side of Hyde Park in London – at that time, a place for the upper-classes to be seen. Bond Street is a fashionable shopping area of London.
[2] Lillie Langtry (1853–1929), nicknamed 'The Jersey Lily', English actress and mistress of the Prince of Wales.
[3] Lady Monckton, née Maria Louisa Long (1837–1920), English actress, wife of Sir John Monckton, Town Clerk of London, and mother of Lionel, writer and composer of musical theatre. The Vanbrughs: the English actresses Violet (1867–1942) and her sister Irene (1872–1949).
[4] The 1737 Theatres Act was politically motivated to impose formal control on actors, by categorising them as 'rogues and vagabonds' unless they were members of a recognised theatre company. The 1737 Theatres Act also introduced censorship of the drama, through the office of the Lord Chamberlain; this censorship was only removed in 1968. While it is a common myth in the profession, there is no evidence to suggest that Irving's influence changed the legal status of actors.
[5] The young Princess May (1867–1953) became Queen Mary to George V in 1910; he was Duke of York when they married in 1893. His brother, Albert ('Eddie'), died in the flu pandemic which swept Britain in the winter of 1891–2.
[6] Fashionable horse-drawn carriages – four-wheeled vehicles with two seats facing each other, drawn by pairs of high-quality horses.

4. The St James's Theatre in London as it looked in the 1890s. **(Alfred Ellis)**

in: the Prince of Wales began surrounding himself with rich commoners, especially Jewish men – Lipton the grocer, the Sassoons – anybody, in fact, who could pay his card debts.[7] There was the Great Baccarat Scandal that rocked the throne![8]

Motor cars were coming in and they looked like horseless carriages, for they had no bonnets yet. They were perpetually breaking down to the irreverent joy of the bus drivers. Those buses! Two horses, straw on the floor in winter and garden seats on top. The drivers were masters of biting wit. One morning, I was on the top because there was no room inside on account of it pouring with rain. We met a funeral. The driver turned his head over his shoulder to me and said: 'Good day for planting out!'

The only theatres playing 'legitimate' were the Lyceum, Haymarket, St James's, Criterion, Court, Avenue, Garrick, Strand, Terry's and The Comedy.[9] Augustin Daly, the American impresario, had just built and opened Daly's in Leicester Square,[10] but Tree had not yet built Her Majesty's.[11] Compare that with the list today![12]

---

[7] This reference to Judaism and its connections with money, money-lending and business was quite typical of the casual anti-Semitism of British middle-class opinion, and taken for granted until after World War Two, when the horrors of the Nazi concentration camps were revealed by Allied forces.

[8] A scandal in which the Prince of Wales (later Edward VII) became embroiled. It was revealed that he had taken part in an illegal card game (baccarat) for money in 1890. He was forced to appear as a witness in court the following year when one of the players sued for slander after being accused of cheating.

[9] Her roll call here is exclusively of London theatres – there were, of course, many regional playhouses (such as The Grand in Leeds) presenting 'legitimate' work. By the time she came to write her memoir (1949), this London list had grown to some 53. J. P. Wearing, *The London Stage 1940–49: A Calendar of Plays and Players*, (Metuchen, N.J.: Scarecrow Press, 1991).

[10] Augustin Daly (1838–1899) built and opened Daly's Theatre in New York in 1879 and later came to London. The foundation stone of Daly's Theatre just off Leicester Square was laid in October 1891 and it opened on 27 June 1893 with Shakespeare's *The Taming of the Shrew*.

[11] Herbert Beerbohm Tree (1853–1917), English actor and later theatre manager and producer. He opened Her Majesty's in 1897.

[12] Listings in *The Times* on 1 January 1949 give details for performances at the following London theatres: Adelphi,

5. 'GA' – George Alexander. (Hulton Archive/Getty Images)

Such, then, was the setting when I made my debut on the London stage. It was the golden age of the actor-manager: he was an autocrat, ran his own theatre, engaged his own company, produced the plays himself (very seldom more than two a year unless he suffered occasional 'short runs' or total failures).

By the end of each July, the theatres were closed (or sub-let) until November. August was given up to holidays and September and October to the Grand Tour to 'first class' provincial towns in the UK (as opposed to 'second-class towns' to which the *real* touring companies were strictly confined). So the working year comprised eleven months, broken up into various engagements or periods of resting, plus six weeks' rehearsal without pay when engaged for a new play and the holiday month at one's own cost.

Thus, after paying Miss Thorne's £26 fee and keeping myself at Margate for five months at £2 a week, that is what I faced (without knowing it) when I presented myself at the St James's stage door on that October morning in 1891 with £30 in my pocket.

I was ushered on to the stage to find a rehearsal in progress. George Alexander, the actor-manager, shook hands and said: 'You'd better go and sit in the stalls.' I did so, feeling rather lost. Except for Miss Marion Terry, I did not know the name of a soul on stage. They were all very chic and didn't look like professionals. Was this the *milieu* Ellen Terry thought I was fitted for?

After I had sat there for a little while, Miss Terry left the stage and, coming through the slips,[13] made straight for me. She sat down beside me and said: 'You have come to join us, haven't you? I hope you will be very happy. You'll soon find

Aldwych, Ambassadors, Apollo, Cambridge, Casino, Coliseum, Comedy, Covent Garden, Criterion, Drury Lane, Duchess, Duke of York's, Fortune, Garrick, Globe, Haymarket, Hippodrome, His Majesty's, Lyric, New, Old Vic, Palace, Palladium, People's Palace, Phoenix, Piccadilly, Playhouse, Prince of Wales, Prince's, Sadler's Wells, St James's, St Martin's, Saville, Savoy, Scala, Stoll (Kingsway), Strand, Vaudeville, Victoria Palace, Westminster, Whitehall, Winter Garden, Wyndham's.

[13] The side of the stage where the actors stand before entering.

your feet you know.' The Terry touch again: so gracious and such charm! Then a voice said: 'Your cue, Miss Terry, please!' and she fled.

Next a man came who said he was the stage manager and his name was Shone.[14] 'Here are two understudy parts, Miss Dolan. Please be in the theatre at 7.30 tonight and remain until after the first act. Then you can go home.' And with that he, too, fled. By two o'clock, rehearsal was over and everybody melted away, so I supposed I was dismissed too until 7.30. I went off to find the lodgings I had been told of in Kensington Crescent and settled myself in with my two precious understudy roles - a matter of a few lines.

At 7.30, I was at the stage door again. Everybody was dressing and I hung about back-stage till the curtain went up. *The Idler* was drawing to the close of its phenomenal run.[15] I was very keen to see Maude Millet who had taken the town by storm in the *ingénue* part, so I crept into the OP (Opposite Prompt) corner and stood watching the play, entranced. What finished acting! It was a small cast and only Miss Millet, George Alexander, Miss Terry and Lady Monckton as the Dowager struck me as 'the real thing'. The others simply played themselves, although quite perfectly. Maude Millet was immense – every line in her part a laugh, which kept the house rocking. Hers was the only role I felt I could have ventured to play.

After I'd watched the entire play from my corner for three nights, Shone came to me: 'What are you doing here?! Don't you know that no-one is allowed on the stage except those concerned in a scene?! Please wait in one of the dressing rooms.' I apologised and crept upstairs.

Three days later, he was waiting for me when I arrived, but this time grinning from ear to ear. 'Mr Alexander missed you in the OP corner the last two nights. He says you are to go where you like in the theatre and only wishes the other young folk would show so much keen interest.' So I was reinstated in my corner and never left it till the curtain fell on the last night of *The Idler* – 6 November.

Meanwhile, I attended daily rehearsals of *Lord Anerley* on the stage itself as understudy to a member of the cast.[16] Miss Terry introduced me to everyone and they were very nice and polite. On 7 November, *Lord Anerley* went into the bill. I was given the leading part to understudy as well, but the thing only ran for five weeks – it was fore-doomed from the first night – and another play went into rehearsal almost at once. On 30 December, *Forgiveness* was produced, but that only ran for seven weeks.[17] These must have been terrible blows to Alexander after the wild success of his first venture into management and I think this was the reason why he never again gave a chance to a dramatist who had not already 'arrived'. Then his luck changed ... and mine too.

I was told to attend the reading of a new play next morning. It was Oscar Wilde's first, *Lady Windermere's Fan,* and Wilde read it himself to the company. I

---

[14] Robert V. Shone, Alexander's stage and business manager.

[15] *The Idler*, a 'melodrama of the drawing-room' by the Australian-born dramatist, C. Haddon Chambers, opened at the St James's on 26 February, 1891, after having been turned down by Beerbohm Tree and John Hare. 'I was beginning to think that playwriting was not all it was set up to be as a career,' wrote Chambers, 'when one day a brilliant and charming lady from America, Elizabeth Marbury, requested a sight of the manuscript, and within a few weeks I was making the first of my thirty visits to New York.' The play made its first appearance on 11 November 1890 at the Lyceum Theatre in New York under the management of the American impresario, Daniel Frohman. Chambers directed the piece himself. Roger Neill, *Haddon Chambers and the Long Arm of Neglect* (article, *Quadrant* magazine, July/August, 2008).

[16] *Lord Anerley* by Mark Quinton and Henry Hamilton (first performed at St James's November 1891). The cast included Ben Webster, and Gertrude Kingston, as well as Marion Terry, Alexander and Arthur Bourchier. Mullin, *Victorian Plays*, 208.

[17] *Forgiveness* by J. Comyns Carr (first performed at St James's, 30 December 1891).

6. *Lady Windermere's Fan*, a big break for George Alexander in 1892 and a small one for 'Miss W Dolan' as Rosalie.

felt sure there was to be a part in it for me. Acts I, II, III – nothing so far. Then, in the last act, Rosalie, Lady Windermere's maid, has a short scene with her mistress – about half a dozen lines. That was me! I saw at once it had some value. I had to say: 'I could not find Her Ladyship's fan anywhere,' nor could she tell me where she'd left it without compromising herself. The little scene was integral to the plot and focused attention for three minutes on the newcomer. I also had a walk-on as a guest in Act III. The play was an overwhelming success and ran for nine months: from 22 February to 3 December 1892.[18]

I had, of course, lost no time in telling Ellen Terry of my engagement and she regularly invited me to visit her home at Barkston Gardens in Kensington. She was always 'at home' on Thursday afternoons and I rarely missed one, but now that I was free of rehearsals all day, I would drop in of a morning on her daughter, Edy, and we would go off together.[19] There were occasional red-letter days when Ellen Terry would take us driving with her in her open carriage perhaps to have her photograph taken or do some shopping or drop us somewhere.

---

[18] A.E.W. Mason gives the opening night as 20 February 1892. Peter Raby argues that it is in *Lady Windermere's Fan* that Wilde 'first found his authentic voice as a playwright.' Raby (ed), 'Introduction,' *The Importance of Being Earnest and Other Plays* (Oxford: Clarendon Pres, 1995), viii. Raby points to the masterly control Wilde exercised over theatrical conventions, and notes the likely influence of plays such as Chambers' *The Idler* on Wilde's manipulation of comic and melodramatic convention. 'Wilde's Comedies of Society,' in Peter Raby (ed), *The Cambridge Companion to Oscar Wilde* (Cambridge: Cambridge University Press, 1997), 144.

[19] Edith Craig (1869–1947), known as 'Edy', English actress, daughter of Ellen Terry. She became a theatre director and producer and early pioneer of the women's suffrage movement. Among the biographies of her are Katharine Cockin, *Edith Craig (Dramatic Lives),* (Continuum International Publishing Group, 1998), and Eleanor Adlard (ed), *Edy – Recollections of Edith Craig*, (Frederick Muller, 1949).

7. Florence Alexander, 'Mrs GA', who did much to uphold the style and sophistication for which the St James's became renowned. **(Hulton Archive/Getty Images)**

Sometimes Edy and I would spend a morning behind the scenes at the Lyceum if no rehearsal was going on.[20] Ellen Terry's dressing room was vast, Irving's quite a lot smaller with a shabby looking-glass on the table. He'd had it from his earliest days and would use no other. We saw the great wardrobe with its thousands of costumes, the women stitching away at repairs; the huge Green Room to which only important members of the cast were ever admitted; the great stage with its proscenium seventy feet high. It was all full of interest and really quite thrilling.

Someone told me that now I was in the bill at the St James's and therefore an accredited actress, I could pass into the theatres on my card. 'My card?' 'Yes, your professional card.' So I hastily had calling cards printed with my name and the St James's address on them and began a round of the theatres.

The only drawback to being on the stage was that I could so seldom go to see fellow actors perform. But now, and during those dreadful intervals of 'resting', I managed to see a good deal on my card: the Kendals, Hare,[21] Tree, Wyndham and Ada Rehan at Daly's new theatre.[22] Also, in the course of time, some performances

---

[20] The greatest of the London theatres at the time, situated just off the Strand. Managed from 1878 by Henry Irving.

[21] John Hare (1844–1921), English actor, and later manager of the Garrick Theatre.

[22] Ada Rehan was born in Ireland in 1859 and was taken to the United States when very young. She joined Daly's company when he opened his theatre in New York in 1879 and continued to work with him until his death twenty years later. 'Under his guidance, Rehan quickly became the finest and probably the most beloved of all younger comediennes.' *Oxford Companion to American Theatre* (Oxford: Oxford University Press, 2004). As well as excelling

Winifred Dolan
S.t James's Theatre 1891.

8. 'My first professional photo was on sale in the shop.' The young actress at the start of her St James's career. **(V&A Images/Theatre Collections)**

from farther afield: Bernhardt, Duse,[23] Grasso and his Sicilian Players,[24] a Russian company in a pogrom play and, when Ibsen became the craze, productions of *The Master Builder* and *The Wild Duck*.[25]

After having had a snoop round the Lyceum, I thought the St James's seemed a small theatre (though, it must be said, much larger than the Criterion, Court and Comedy). The Earl of Kilmorey owned it and George Alexander was his lessee. By the by, you're going to read a lot about Alexander from now on, so for brevity's sake I will start to refer to him by his sobriquet, GA. The theatre was beautifully run off-stage by his wife, Florence (Mrs GA!): she supervised the furnishings and appointments of all the modern interior sets, the ladies' dresses and front of house. She generally occupied her box ready to entertain bigwigs, for our clientele were of the elite.[26]

In the foyer, a huge display of flowers filled up the space between the two little flights of stairs leading up to the Dress Circle; another staircase led to a bar upstairs. Here the men in the audience retired between acts to smoke a cigarette. Ladies did not crunch chocolates or balance tea-trays on their knees in the stalls – that would have been the equivalent of sucking oranges in the pit at Drury Lane. In fact, it was all very chic. We had a small Green Room to which all playing a part had access and it was here, on matinee days, that Mrs Evans, the Wardrobe Mistress cum Housekeeper – daintily aproned - would dispense afternoon tea to us between Acts II and III.

'The *Fan*' had now been playing to packed houses for a month and the advanced bookings were so heavy that GA put on two matinees a week and on 30 March, a *lever de rideau* by Frith called *Midsummer Day*,[27] casting me as the juvenile lead in it. There were only four characters: my parents, my lover and myself. It was a very commonplace trifle offering nothing to any of us to make much use of – just straight acting. However, it was a part at last (you could hardly call Rosalie in 'The *Fan*' a part) and up to then I had begun to feel rather heart-sick. Six months at a guinea a week and as mum as the grave! How long, too, was my £30 going to last?

I opened the *Daily Telegraph* next morning with trembling hands. What was Clement Scott going to say of his *protégée*? I had no need of worry:

> Miss Winifred Dolan is a young actress of great promise. She has pathos, is natural and she has just that welcome earnestness that must, in the long run, beat down all the frivolity and insincerity that, though showy, are not so abiding.

in classic comedy, including Shakespeare and Sheridan, she was equally at home in the newer comedies presented by Daly. She retired from the stage in 1906 and died in New York in 1916. Biography: William Winter, *Ada Rehan: A Study* (privately printed for Daly, 1891, but reprinted Reprint Services Corp., 2007).

[23] Eleanora Duse (1859–1924), the greatest Italian actress of the day.

[24] Giovanni Grasso (1873–1930), leading Sicilian actor.

[25] Henrik Ibsen (1828–1906), Norwegian playwright. His work was championed by a select group of English and Irish critics and theatre practitioners at the vanguard of the 'New Drama' from the 1870s. 'Ibsenism' came to signify the *avant garde* in London theatre at the end of the century, and his work was connected with radical critiques of Victorian politics and morality, particular the rights of women, and the role of marriage in society. Chief amongst campaigners for Ibsen's plays were the critic, William Archer, the writer Eleanor Marx (daughter of Karl Marx) and the actress and writer, Elizabeth Robins, and the actress-manager, Janet Achurch.

[26] In notes at the end of A. E. W. Mason's *Sir George Alexander and the St James' Theatre*, Florence Alexander gave her own account of her duties. 'First nights at the St James' Theatre were great events (…) I sat in my box sick with anxiety, and between the acts I used to put on an apron and go behind the scenes to place all the little things on the stage myself until the men got used to it. I arranged the flowers; in those days we had so much detail, and I loved to make things look real. I ordered the gowns to suit the decorations of the scene so that nothing clashed or was ugly. Alec [Alexander] gave me the large sum of £5 a week for my work, and I think I was very cheap at the price.'

[27] *Midsummer Day* by Walter Frith, a curtain raiser for *Lady Windermere's Fan* (March, 1892).

The *Standard* said I played my role in *Midsummer Day* 'naturally and gracefully'. The *Sunday Chronicle* shared Mr Scott's view of me as an actress of great promise. I breathed again![28]

That night I was mercilessly chaffed by the company who dubbed me 'the Pet of the *Daily Telegraph*' (read Clement Scott!) That second night, as the fates would have it, I dried for a few seconds (and this time it was the lover who prompted *me*). As I came off stage, I ran into GA in the wings. Dismayed, I said: 'Oh were you in prompt? I dried.'

He laughed and said 'Wait until you act with Ellen Terry and then you can talk of drying. You're very good and I've just told my Acting Manager to double your salary from last night.'

Before I could properly thank him he'd gone to dress.

While I am indulging in theatrical pitfalls, let me give you a variant of drying. It's called 'fluffing'. An actress of the old school, Miss Fanny Coleman,[29] had joined us for 'The *Fan*'. She played the Duchess superbly. Miss Graves[30] played her daughter and had nothing to say except 'Yes, Mama' *ad nauseam* until one night she said 'No, Mama', and brought the house down.

In another scene, the Duchess calls on Lady Windermere to tell her the gossip about her husband's (supposed) goings-on. Suddenly she remembers her daughter's presence. 'Agatha darling, go and sit on the terrace and look at the sunset.' 'Yes, Mama.' This particular night Miss C. said: 'Agatha darling, go and sit on the sunset and look …' Horror-struck, she stopped short. The house rocked. Another time, I heard Marion Terry tell a magnificent flunkey to carry the tent into the buns. He nearly dropped the tray.

I was now earning £3/2/9 a week – that is, two guineas plus 15/6 for the first matinee and 5/3 for the second.[31] It was enough to live on, I was in the bill with a part, I had had a good Press and my first professional photo was on sale in the shop. I felt I had climbed another rung of that ladder and for the moment was content. My only regret was that my mother had come to see me in the part of Rosalie. I wished she had waited until now. While my mother was with me, Ellen Terry gave us seats to see her as Beatrice in *Much Ado;* indeed, she always lent me her box whenever my mother came to town and I often used to pop into it to see an act or two when I was on early or very late in the St James's bill – flying to and fro in a hansom.

During a successful run, it was the custom to give 'flying matinees' at the Crystal Palace and Brighton. I had my first experience of these that season of 1892. It was a hectic business getting back to central London with just an hour to spare to snatch a meal of sorts in time to appear in the evening show, but I enjoyed it. Apart from anything else, it meant extra pay!

Gordon Craig wanted me to play Kate Hardcastle to his Marlow in *She Stoops to Conquer*[32] if Miss Thorne would let us do it at Margate in the holiday recess. She agreed and also asked me to play lead in *The Porter's Knot*.[33] So when

---

[28] All the reviews quoted in this memoir have been cut from the original newspapers, and pasted in to the manuscript, presumably by Dolan herself.
[29] Fanny Coleman (1840–1919), English actress who made her debut in a walk-on at the Haymarket in 1857 and, late in her career, specialised in elderly titled ladies. On her death, one of the obituaries said she would be remembered as 'one of those rare old ladies of the stage who could combine sweetness, broad humour and dignity in a way that seemed perfectly easy and natural but really needed a lifetime of art.' The *Argus*, Melbourne, 24 May 1919.
[30] Laura Graves (1870–1925), English actress.
[31] The decimal equivalent is £3.14.
[32] *She Stoops to Conquer* by Oliver Goldsmith (1773).
[33] *The Porter's Knot* by John Oxenford (1858). A serio-comic drama in two acts. 'This little tale abounds in opportunities of pathos, relieved and often deepened by humour', Marston, 1890, 368.

the theatres closed down, the first week in August found us back at the old theatre. Miss Thorne bade us a warm welcome and 'starred' us on the bills – 'Gordon Craig from the Lyceum and Miss Winifred Dolan from the St James's Theatre, London. For Two Weeks Only'.

It was fun and we both got a very flattering reception from 'the quality', who always patronised these extra shows. The rest of the holiday I spent at home seeing old friends again, not forgetting the high school to which I owed so much. On 1 September, I was back in town again to start the tour.

We took with us *The Idler*, Miss Millet playing her old part and 'The *Fan*', including *Midsummer Day*. We opened at The Grand, Islington.[34] I think it was to give us a 'shakedown' before tackling the provinces, for provincial audiences were not to be treated lightly. They offered a cross-section of the people and you had to please all of the people all of the time! The theatres, too, were much larger and required broader treatment to get your effects without losing your London delicacy of touch. We visited Leeds, Manchester, Liverpool, Newcastle, Birmingham, Edinburgh and Glasgow.

We had a special train: two Pullman cars (for gentlemen and ladies), one ordinary coach for the stage staff and trucks for the scenery which were usually tacked on to the usual expresses. We had splendid receptions everywhere and we were back in town the first week in November, re-opening with 'The *Fan*' until a new play could be got ready.

We didn't yet know it, but the next few productions at the St James's would include a runaway success and a complete flop.

---

[34] The Grand in Islington was originally the Philharmonic Hall, which opened in 1860. From 1871, it offered light French operas and can-can girls, which attracted a fashionable male audience. The hall burned down in 1882 and opened the following year as the Grand, designed by Frank Matcham. It burned down again in 1887, was rebuilt in 1888, burned down a third time in 1900, but again rose from the ashes. Until its closure in 1962, the building was variously known as the Empire Islington, the Islington Palace and the Islington Empire. *A History of the County of Middlesex*: Volume 8: Islington and Stoke Newington Parishes (1985), 45–51.

Chapter IV

'Though patience be a tired mare, yet she will plod'
– *King Henry V*

Miss Graves was leaving us and I had every prospect of getting her small parts, but GA came to me rather nervously to tell me that my friend Edy Craig was joining us. 'Ellen Terry has asked me to give her a chance; she's doing nothing at the Lyceum.' And, sure enough, she was cast as 'Mith Hickthon' (with a lisp) in *Liberty Hall* by R. C. Carton,[1] which was put into rehearsal at once – and I understudied *her*! Marion Terry was also in it, playing Blanche Chilworth, and it was about this time that she and I became great friends.

I had started an autograph book and passed it to her so that she could add her name. She kept it for so long that at last I asked her for it. She said: 'I can't find where the quotation comes from – do wait a bit.' Very soon she called me to her dressing room. She had written: 'I would be friends with you and have your love *(Merchant of Venice)*. Marion Terry.'[2] I thanked her warmly but I think the corners of my mouth must have twitched for she said, 'What is it?' I said, laughingly, that I hoped it was true, for I reminded her that it was what Shylock had said to Antonio! How we laughed!

Then she took a little plain gold serpent friendship ring off her finger and gave it to me. 'It's quite true,' she said, we embraced and I've worn it ever since. She was such a dear woman. I had the run of her flat and we used to go about hunting in antique shops: she collected tea caddies.

Edy did not stay long with us and I stepped into her shoes. But I had not *created* the part – it was only valuable as further practice, not for publicity. But one night the Prince of Wales was in the Royal Box and GA as usual presented the leading players. Shone told me afterwards: 'His Nibs said to the Guvnor: "You've got a new member in your company, the lady playing Miss Hickson. She's very clever."'

We had a 'flying matinee' to the Crystal Palace and when we got there it was to find there was a poultry show on. The clucking and crowing were deafening. GA was furious with his staff for booking such a date. Orders were given that every door was to be shut and a sentinel placed at each. All went well until Act III at the end of the great love scene when GA wins his lady. At the exact psychological moment, a cock crowed. The audience was convulsed. 'Damn that bird,' snarled poor GA, and the curtain was hurriedly brought down.

---

[1] *Liberty Hall*, a four-act play by R.C.Carton (1892). 'The wit of the dialogue and the humours of the low comedy parts, equally with the beautiful acting of Miss Marion Terry, Mr George Alexander [and] Mr George Righton, whose quaint pathetic and picturesque sketch of Todman brought the stuffiness of musty volumes across the footlights, ensured it a long career.' *A Chronicle of the St James's Theatre from its Origin in 1835*, (publisher and author unknown, 1900), 23.
[2] Act 1, Scene iii, line 138.

Around this time in 1893, a tiny cloud appeared on the social horizon which presently developed into a veritable cloudburst. A journalist, W. T. Stead, started a purity crusade.[3] Ugly rumours were afloat of immorality in high circles. Even Mr Gladstone's name was dragged in. The Grand Old Man used to walk home after a late-night sitting at the House and was known to get into conversation with prostitutes, although this was with a view to converting them from their ways.[4]

Several public men were accused by the police – on insufficient evidence – of irregular behaviour and GA was one of them. One night he left his house late to post an urgent letter. A woman accosted him and he gave the poor soul half a crown whereupon a young policeman pounced on him to arrest him for soliciting. GA protested furiously, so the PC took his name and address and the next day he received a summons to appear at a police court.

The whole profession was up in arms and when GA appeared in court it was packed with his brother actor-managers, critics and playwrights to testify on his behalf. Pinero was in court and a play of his was running entitled *The Benefit Of The Doubt*.[5] The charge was dismissed in three minutes, the PC censured and then the magistrate – a man noted for his facetious wit – smiled across at Pinero and said: 'I think we must give him the benefit of the doubt.' There was laughter in court, of course, but the words, reported in the press the next day, gave a very different impression to the reading public who had not been present. It could have spelled ruin for GA.

That night, the Duke and Duchess of Fife were in the Royal Box with Mrs GA, and the stalls crammed with the leading lights of society, with the pit and gallery also packed to the limit. When GA made his entrance, white as a sheet, the whole house rose to its feet and cheered and clapped and waved programmes for ten minutes. A voice from the gallery shouted: 'You're all right, George. We *know* you.' Tears streamed down GA's cheeks (and we, the rest of the cast, were in much the same situation). It had been touch and go. But what a rally of the public on behalf of their slandered favourite known for his unblemished life!

Liberty Hall had been running for nearly six months and another play was on the *tapis* – it was *The Second Mrs Tanqueray* and, as it turned out, it was going to make history.[6] It had been written for John Hare, but he'd turned it down; GA risked it. But the author, Pinero, would not have Marion Terry to play Paula. He said she was too 'good'. He wanted an intrinsically bad woman with better possibilities in her make-up, but essentially past social redemption as a respectable married woman. Now Marion had played a 'fallen woman' quite beautifully in 'The *Fan*', but there she'd been a society woman – a lady born – who had left her husband and child for

---

[3] William Thomas Stead (1849–1912), journalist and moral crusader who died on the *Titanic*. Stead was editor of the *Pall Mall Gazette*, and from 4 July 1885 he published the results of his investigations into the trafficking of young girls into prostitution in London, in a series of sensational articles called 'The Maiden Tribute of Modern Babylon'. Judith Walkowitz argues that the political effects of Stead's articles were 'startling', including reform of the age of consent laws, and – as Oscar Wilde was to find to his peril – hardened up legislation against 'indecent acts' between consenting males. *City of Dreadful Delight: Narratives of Sexual Danger in Late-Victorian London* (Chicago: University of Chicago Press, 1992), 82–3.

[4] Gladstone had first embarked on his work of rescuing and rehabilitating London prostitutes in 1840.

[5] The narrative seems to have jumped forward a little here as the incident involving George Alexander occurred during 1895 – when Pinero's *The Benefit of The Doubt* was playing at the Comedy Theatre.

[6] *The Second Mrs Tanqueray* by Arthur Wing Pinero (1893). 'Besides making a reputation for Mrs Patrick Campbell and confirming Alexander's position at the St James's, this play placed Pinero firmly in the ranks of the Society dramatists.' George Rowell, *The Victorian Theatre 1792–1914*, (Cambridge: Cambridge University Press 1956), 113–4.

9. George Alexander with Mrs Patrick Campbell in *The Second Mrs Tanqueray* (1893).
'GA hated her, so to see him play love scenes with her was a joy!'
(Hulton Archive/Getty Images)

a lover: a *déclassée*. This was a very different prospect to Paula in *The Second Mrs Tanqueray*, who was a *demi-mondaine*.[7]

Marion Terry was a 'comedy' not a 'great' actress – she could never convey vice across the footlights: people would have smiled, albeit affectionately. It was a cruel blow to her, but did her no lasting harm. Pinero was right and the box office is the final referee! The theatres were scoured in the search for an actress to fit the type. At last GA found her at the Adelphi Theatre – of all unlikely places – in a full-blooded melodrama in which she played the villainess. It was Mrs Patrick Campbell.[8]

The new play was put into rehearsals and they were stormy – to put it mildly. The lady was temperamental and resented being told what to do. Pinero produced his own plays and was a genius: he knew every gesture and look to use to convey his meaning. A morning came when the lady threw up her part – or rather she threw

---

[7] *Déclassée:* a woman of inferior social status; *demi-mondaine:* a class of woman considered to be in an unrespectable social position, e.g. the kept mistress of a society man.

[8] Mrs Patrick Campbell (1865–1940), one of the most successful English stage actresses of the period. The play at the Adelphi was *The Black Domino* by G. R. Sims and Robert Buchanan, of which it was said: 'She acted creditably in this role, but there was nothing great in her work. Her death scene in the last act, however, impressed Mr Pinero greatly and that scene procured her the chance to play Paula [in *The Second Mrs Tanqueray*], which has resulted in raising her from comparative obscurity to the high position which she now occupies on the London stage.' *New York Times* 18 June 1893, 12. Biographies of Mrs Patrick Campbell include Alan Dent, *Mrs Patrick Campbell*, (Museum Press, 1961) and Margot Peters, *Mrs Pat: Biography of Mrs Patrick Campbell*, (Bodley Head, 1984).

it down, stamped on it and walked out. I think GA must have come to the rescue; anyway, Mrs Pat turned up again next morning.

Pinero was very patient and very polite but adamant. Both he and GA were as nervous as kittens as to the reception the piece would get; it was a daring novelty and, for the period, strong meat. But the story was handled in such a masterly fashion that only Victorian prudes could have found fault. It was a great work of art. The most amazing proof was that the Kendals bought the American rights and toured it in the United States.

On 27 May 1893, the curtain rose on the greatest success of George Alexander's career. It ran until 21 April 1894 – eleven months! It had a wonderful cast and I was given two parts to understudy. William Archer, a great critic and literary man, wrote:

> I wonder if Mr Pinero himself quite realises what an immeasurable advance he has made on all his former works? He has written a play which Dumas might sign without a blush. Here we can praise without reservation. In Mrs Patrick Campbell, Mr Alexander has laid his hand upon the very woman for the part of Paula. Her performance was as novel and unconventional as the character itself and her triumphal success was thoroughly deserved.'[9]

The Press were *almost* unanimous. The one exception was dear old Clement Scott, who fulminated to the amazement of all concerned. In addition, an anguished back-bencher in the House of Commons asked the Home Secretary 'whether, in view of the depraved character of some of the plays now being acted in London theatres, the Government would consider placing their licensing under the control of the London County Council.'[10] The Home Secretary replied that he was satisfied that morality was safe in the hands of the Lord Chamberlain's censorship.

A publication called *Great Thoughts* asked Mr W. T. Stead's opinion. He gave it thus:

> As I have never been in a theatre in my life, I am not in a position to speak with any authority. But if Mr Clement Scott is right, I think my parents did well to inculcate upon me from boyhood to avoid the theatre as the pit of hell.[11]

Well!

The marriage of Princess Mary (May) of Teck to her cousin, Prince George, Duke of York, was the social event of that summer of 1893. The back of GA's smart little house in Park Row looked on to the park and he was kind enough to invite me to see the Royal couple drive with their escort to the station on the way to their honeymoon. That night at the theatre, the neighbouring boxes to the Royal Box were

---

[9] William Archer (1856–1924), drama critic and champion of the work of Ibsen. It is not clear whether he is referring to Alexandre Dumas *père* (1802–1870) or *fils* (1824–1895), French authors and playwrights. The quotations are from a review of *The Second Mrs Tanqueray* by William Archer in *World,* 31 May 1893.

[10] The backbencher was probably Samuel Smith, the Liberal MP for Flintshire, who was campaigning around this time about what he saw as depravity in the theatre and 'the spread of demoralising literature'.

[11] It is possible this quote appeared, in fact, in the *Review of Reviews*, a periodical which Stead co-founded in January 1890. Written almost exclusively by him, it contained dozens of magazine and book reviews, a commentary on world events and a profile of a current celebrity. *Great Thoughts* was the evangelical publication in which Clement Scott gave his inflammatory views on actresses (see Chapter VII).

all thrown into one for the Prince and Princess of Wales and all the Kings and minor Royals who'd attended the wedding. It was a great honour that St James's had been chosen.

A few hours before the curtain went up, I was told I must go on in the part of Lady George Orreyed, as Miss Elsie Chester was indisposed.[12] I had had no personal rehearsal, only the close watching of the production itself. I was nervous, but so elated – a high comedy part at last, only on in one act, but the prized Act III and a scene with Mrs Patrick Campbell herself. A plum!

My name was not, of course, on the satin programmes in the Royal Box and when GA took Mrs Pat to be presented, 'His Nibs' said: 'The young lady who is taking Miss Chester's part tonight, is she not the young lady who played that small part in *Liberty Hall*?' 'Yes, sir.' 'She is very, very clever.' One more royal 'very' than last time and all very nice, but not much use to me: I'd had no press, and it was recognition by the Great British Press that I wanted. Still, it was a thrilling experience from all points of view and our scene went to continual laughter and running applause.

The next play was *The Masqueraders* by Henry Arthur Jones.[13] I hated it: it was sheer melodrama decked out in West End clothes. Mr Jones's baronets and ladies were 'stock' figures. He was an excellent and established playwright but to my mind did not know the *beau monde*. Mrs Pat simply made sport at rehearsals and behaved abominably. One day she started looking about for something on the floor. The rehearsal was stopped. 'Have you lost something, Mrs Campbell?' 'I'm looking for the aitches that Mr Jones has dropped.' Cruel. GA hated her, so to see him play love scenes with her was a joy!

She took it out on him by standing in the wings during his own scenes tittering audibly. At last he sent his dresser to her with a note: 'Mr Alexander's compliments, but will Mrs Campbell please cease standing in the wings laughing at him?'

Back came her reply: 'Mrs Campbell's compliments. Mr Alexander is quite mistaken: she does not stand in the wings laughing at him, she waits until she gets home.'

Poor GA. The lady was not loved or approved of by the St James's company. *The Masqueraders* was produced on 28 April 1894 and ran and ran and ran. I had only the understudy of the second lead.

GA asked me if I would come to his house in the mornings for a week or two to write his letters (he had no secretary yet). I accepted, no knowing what it would lead to. One morning he handed me a script. 'I want you to read this play and tell me what you think of it.' I was astonished. I assured him I couldn't judge a play by reading it. He had no use for diffidence and insisted. 'Take it home, read it and let me know what you think of it.'

---

[12] Elsie Chester (d.1937), English actress who later became a drama teacher at RADA. John Gielgud said of his time there in the 1920s: 'I never worked with Elsie Chester, a redoubtable old actress who was still giving classes at the Academy though (like Sarah Bernhardt) she had only one leg and was reputed to fling her crutch at inefficient pupils.' (Recollections in *RADA, The Magazine*, 1993.)

[13] *The Masqueraders* by Henry Arthur Jones (1894), a play 'Jones designed for Alexander and Mrs Patrick Campbell to follow up their triumph in *The Second Mrs Tanqueray*, thereby measuring his talent against Pinero's'. George Rowell, *The Victorian Theatre 1792-1914*, (Cambridge: Cambridge University Press, 1956), 120. 'Again the critics sounded the trumpets of success, again the public responded with alacrity and again the theatre was packed during a run which hardly fell short of that of *Tanqueray*.' *A Chronicle of the St James's Theatre from its Origin in 1835* (publisher and author unknown, 1900), 25.

I read it and found to my horror I did not like it. That is to say, as a play. What was I to do? I took it back. 'Well?' said GA.

I replied: 'It's not fair to ask such an inexperienced person as I am to …'

'What do you think of it?'

So I plunged. 'I think that, as literature, it is outstandingly good. I think the plot is dull. I think the drunken scene in Act III is a mistake. I think it – well – I think it won't act.'

'Oh,' said GA with a grin, 'I'm going to produce it. It's by Henry James.'[14] Henry James! I had put my foot in it.

To jump forward a little: when the play *Guy Domville* was produced in 1895, the first night was a painful experience for all concerned.[15] The house was restless right from the first act. Then came Miss Pauncefort,[16] who was an enormously large woman in an exaggerated crinoline. It was so exaggerated, in fact, that she couldn't get through the door and had to enter sideways. By now, the house was out of hand – the audience were delirious with laughter and when GA spoke the tag to bring down the final curtain, 'I am the last of the Domvilles,' a wag in the gallery fervently exclaimed: 'Thank God!' It was a dreadful fiasco. The press were kind to the great writer, but unanimous that the drunken scene was a blot on the piece. It was cut out on the second night. The play had a short run and soon came off.

That, then, was my first brush with an American celebrity. I was about to have another.

---

[14] Henry James (1843–1916), American-born author who spent much of his life in England. By 1893, James had established a reputation as a novelist, travel writer and critic.

[15] In *Sir George Alexander and the St James' Theatre,* A.E.W. Mason says that on the first night of *Guy Domville* there was 'an explosion of cat-calls and boos and hisses as was seldom heard, even in those days when first-night disturbances were not uncommon.' The third part of Leon Edel's five-volume biography, *Henry James, The Middle Years 1881–95,* (Lippincott Williams & Wilkins, 1962) covers in detail the debacle of *Guy Domville* and the effect it had on James's subsequent work.

[16] Probably Claire Pauncefort (d. 1924), English actress on stage and in silent films.

Chapter V

'Past and to come seem best; things present worst'
King Henry IV Part 2

Knowing beforehand that there would be no part for me in *Guy Domville*, and sick of always under-studying, I was determined to make a fresh break. After we returned from the autumn tour of 1894, I asked the American impresario Augustin Daly for an interview. He inquired what salary I was getting and said: 'Well, I'll engage you on $15 a week, but I can't promise you a part. You must make yourself useful.' $15 was about £3 then – a come-down, but anything to get out of the rut I was in. I accepted.

I was with him at Leicester Square for six months and it was a queer experience in many ways. Daly was an autocrat and his leading lady, Ada Rehan, like royalty. Each of them had a black dresser – Sambo and Mammy.[1] Only those with standing in the company could address either of the principals unless spoken to. And, *entre nous*, the man spat on the carpets!

Daly must have carried with him at least two score men and women to walk on and understudy. Many of them never spoke a word on the stage in three years. A number of them married in the company, while the families of some of the girls apparently followed them everywhere so that they could live at home wherever they were.

It took me some time to learn all this. One night, Miss Rehan dropped her handkerchief. I picked it up and handed it to her. She threw it down again. I had taken a liberty, I suppose. But the rank and file took me to their hearts; they were dear folk. There were three other English actors in the company, including Arthur Bourchier and Vi Vanbrugh, to whom he was engaged.[2]

The bill was often changed. I was a fairy, complete with electric wand, in Tennyson's *The Foresters*,[3] with music by Sir Arthur Sullivan (who conducted on the first night) and I danced in a minuet in *The School For Scandal*, in which Daly

---

[1] 'Sambo' and 'Mammy' were terms derived from Black Minstrel shows, which in turn were based on the racist stereotypes imposed on enslaved African-Americans by their white American owners. For a discussion of the impact of the stereotypes of minstrelsy, see Hazel Waters, *Racism on the Victorian Stage: Representation of Slavery and the Black Character* (Cambridge: Cambridge University Press, 2007).

[2] Arthur Bourchier (1863–1927), English actor and manager, who married Violet Vanbrugh in 1894. She had toured with the Kendals and appeared at the Lyceum with Irving and Terry, winning acclaim for her performance as Anne Boleyn in King Henry VIII. In 1893, she acted with Bourchier in *Love in Tandem* at Daly's. When Bourchier took over the lease of the Royalty in 1895, he and Violet Vanbrugh starred in a run of successes that continued when her husband took over the management of the Garrick.

[3] *The Foresters* by Alfred Tennyson, music by Sir Arthur Sullivan (1891). Tennyson reportedly wrote his verse play about Robin Hood and Maid Marian at Augustin Daly's request. Daly, who had met Arthur Sullivan in California, then asked him to write the music and Sullivan composed the nine short numbers which comprise the score. *The Foresters* was first produced in New York in 1892 and was well received; the New York Times described it as 'simple, dainty and interesting' (18 March 1892). It went on to play in seven other American cities. The piece received poor notices in London, however, and had only a short run.

took barbarous liberties, transposing scenes and so on. One poor old actor said to me: 'I just don't know where I am!'

I was given one understudy, Olivia in *Twelfth Night*, and heard no more about it for some weeks until one morning a hansom brought a note to my digs – come at once! I hopped in and when I went on the stage, found five ladies being tested in the part. I went up to Mr Clarke, the stage manager, and said I understood I was under-studying the part. 'There are a lot of you under-studying it.' 'So I see, but that is not our custom in England. I beg to claim the part.' 'Go sit down, please.' I sat down.

The five ladies each said a bit. One was a cockney, another an Italian pseudo-countess with broken English, another couldn't remember her lines. At last Clarke said: 'Say you, Miss, you've a good opinion of yourself. Give us a taste of your quality.' I began the speech 'By the roses of the spring' and after a few lines he stopped me. 'Go upstairs and dress,' he said. And that was that. I was expected to play the part at the matinee that very afternoon.

It was the year of the terrible Spanish flu scourge and Vi Vanbrugh had gone down with it. Now Vi was taller and bigger than I, so her dresser literally tacked her dress on to me and it had a huge train. When I went down to the stage, Mr Daly and Miss Rehan were waiting for me. The orchestra was tuning up and I was sick with nervousness, not to mention discomfort in my clothes.

Daly said, very nicely: 'This is the young lady who is going to play Olivia to your Viola.'

'Well I hope she knows her words,' replied Miss Rehan.

She looked green with fright herself – no wonder, if this was the way unknown understudies were thrown at her! Then a voice said 'Beginners, please!' The overture started and we went to our places. I wore Vi's red wig with long curls falling on my neck on each side of my face and entered reading a book. I got a warm reception, but when I lifted my head from the book to say 'Take the fool away', the audience discovered the 'imposter' and a storm of hisses greeted me.

My heart missed a beat, but then anger cured fright: 'All right,' I thought, 'so these are American manners? I'll teach 'em how St James's acts!' As I made my first exit, they gave me a tremendous round of applause. I'd got them, but it had been an ordeal. It seems they were angry that no announcement had been made that Miss Vanbrugh was not playing. The next scene I had to encounter Miss Rehan as Viola. She dried and I gave her her words. If looks could have killed!

I played the part again that night but the following morning was down with flu myself, perhaps from wearing Vi's clothes. I was very ill for five weeks – delirious and so on. When I went back I was put straight into the part again and when I got my pay envelope at the end of the week it was bursting. The secretary told me that Mr Daly was very pleased with me and wanted me to accept my week's salary of £3 plus £15 for the five weeks I was away ill. That was Daly all over: queer and quixotic. For a UK company it would have been 'no play, no pay.'

They were all very civil to me after that. Mr and Mrs Daly and Miss Rehan were good Catholics: the Pope had sent Daly the Golden Rose.[4] When Daly paid his first visits to London, Ada Rehan took the town by storm with her tantrums in *The Taming Of The Shrew*. She was a perfect comedienne, not pretty but piquante in a lovely way with a voice like honey and perfect diction. Off-stage she was the dowdiest of the dowdy; she was painfully shy and shunned social contacts.

---

[4] A sacred ornament made of pure gold given by Popes as a mark of esteem.

Daly built his theatre in Leicester Square to play six months in London and six months in New York, but he lost money on it, for the waters of oblivion quickly close over a gap of six months in theatre-land. You must always be in that public eye that is so hard to catch. The company were now going home to the United States and Daly sold the theatre to George Edwardes, whose musical comedies (*The Geisha* etc) thenceforth are the only memories associated with it.[5] The theatre eventually closed in 1937.

So now, in 1895, I had to look out for – in theatre slang – another 'shop'. Otho Stuart, a rich dilettante and an old Bensonian, had bought the touring rights of *The Masqueraders* and GA recommended me for second lead.[6] So I was engaged to play the part of the smug Helen at £3 a week. How I hated that tour and that part. Travelling all Sunday, living in theatrical lodgings and with the dullest of all dull companions. We travelled far and wide from Bath to Aberdeen. Of course the seaside and cathedral towns were a joy, but oh, the weather in winter and the grubby theatres!

We had a break of a week at Christmas and then took to the road again. We would usually start about 8.30–9.30am so as to get to the next town early enough to look for lodgings. I was coming back from early Mass one Sunday morning when I met a fellow lodger from another company on the stairs. She said: 'I say, are you a Catholic? You must be very good getting up to early Mass on Sundays. I can't – too tired! But my confessor has given me leave to attend later Mass and go in after the Gospel.' Poor girl, I wondered how long she would keep *that* up. I never got the chance of a late Mass on tour. No, it was a dog's life to live all the year round, speaking the same old lines eight times a week for a year. Deadening to one's art. Mr Stuart treated us well, though; as with the St James's tour, we had two Pullmans while our scenery truck was tacked on to normal trains. But very often we were shunted into a siding for two or three hours, halfway through a journey, to be picked up by a second train to carry us to our destination. We couldn't get out to walk – we were stuck. Again, it was not always possible to book dates in neighbouring towns. One journey was from Eastbourne to Dundee, then back again to Leicester.

I have said I hated my part, but I did get some favourable reviews. A paper in Aberdeen said I laid my cool hand on the fever of the piece as I laid it upon my sister's burning forehead. And the *Hastings Argus* was kind enough to refer to my 'clever natural acting.' There were others and I sent them all to GA.

We had our little excitements now and then on tour. One night a side wing caught fire. I had had a lesson at the St James's, which now stood me in good stead. On that occasion, Marion Terry and another actress were sitting side by side in a garden scene when a leafy border took fire. Marion went on calmly with the scene while men rushed on with great wooden hay-forks to douse the thing down. So I now went on quickly with the scene and the men again came and put it out. Fire in a theatre can mean panic and then God help us all!

There was an actor in the cast, Douglas Gordon, who had a dog, a dachshund, to which he was devoted. Gordon had the role of Archie, the young brother of the hero and it was our job – his and mine – to rescue the heroine, Dulcie, by appealing to the hero's conscience, his honour and all the rest. It was the big scene

---

[5] *The Geisha* (1896), a musical comedy composed by Sidney Jones to a libretto by Owen Hall with lyrics by Harry Greenbank. George Edwardes was later to be involved in the controversy over the licensing of the Empire of Varieties. See Chapter VII.

[6] Otho Stuart (1865–1930), British theatre manager who ran the Adelphi from 1904 to 1908.

in the last act and the three of us had it to ourselves. It was one of those difficult scenes when all the speeches run into each other like interruptions. One night, at the critical moment, the dog walked on. Gordon lost his head, left us and picked up his dog to shove it into the wings. But he forgot there were two or three steps up on to the stage and he threw the little dog down them, which prompted a loud and pitiful yelp. Gordon rushed off to comfort it and the two of us were left to finish the scene alone. I had to combine Gordon's dialogue with my own: 'As Archie says' or 'As Archie would say …' – that kind of thing.

At last the curtain came down. The audience had never moved a muscle. I was showered with compliments and gratitude with the result that next night, pride had a fall. In this same scene, the hero takes Dulcie's wedding ring off her finger and hurls it down a chasm 'off'. He was an astronomer and we were in his observatory. I missed my cue and there was an awful stage wait. The call-boy came rushing to my dressing room which was on the same side as the 'chasm'. To save time, I walked across it. They were not pleased with me on that occasion.

At Bradford, Otho Stuart produced a one-act play by his brother, *Two's Company*.[7] He gave me the woman's part – a lovely high comedy role of a gay young widow. This is one of the notices I got for it:

> The part of Arabella Armstrong was taken by Miss Winifred Dolan, an actress of decided distinction and marked intelligence, formerly a member of the St James's company. Her acting bore evidence not only of careful study but of a natural grace and ready expression which gave vitality to the action of the piece whenever she was on stage.

Flattering – but Stuart only kept the little play on for a week and I never played it again.

Towards the end of the tour, we played at Richmond (Surrey) and Mr and Mrs GA came round afterwards. He said to me: 'Winifred, I'd no idea you could act like that. How would you like to come and play the part with me on tour?'

Now, Stuart was coming out again with a new play and would take me on; also Benson had come to see me and had offered me an engagement when this tour finished. I told GA of these two offers and reminded him his tour only lasted eight weeks.

He said: 'Now, my dear, can't you trust me? I tell you, I had no idea you could act like that' (we see very little of our colleagues' acting when we are playing with them unless actually concerned in scenes together.) Like a fool, I did trust him. Stuart kindly released me and I went back to the St James's. I fancy this was the turning point in my career – and I took the wrong road.

---

[7] *Two's Company* by Percy Andreae (1895).

Chapter VI

'Words, words, words'
– Hamlet

So I was back with the St James's company again and on this Grand Tour in 1895, we were evidently intending to make a splash. There were five plays in our repertoire and two leading ladies, Mrs Patrick Campbell in *The Second Mrs Tanqueray* and *The Masqueraders* and Evelyn Millard engaged for Marion Terry's parts in *The Idler* and *Liberty Hall* and also for lead in the most recent St James's production, *The Triumph of the Philistines*.[1]

I was handed my parts: Helen in *The Masqueraders* (ugh!), 'Mith Hickthon' in *Liberty Hall* and Ellean in '*Tanqueray*'.[2] In addition to the three parts, I was to under-study all five leading roles – eight parts to carry in my head, five of which I might be called upon at a moment's notice to play. It did look as if GA was giving me my chance but not one single understudy rehearsal was called throughout the tour. I have often wondered whether GA knew and countenanced it. Or was Shone, the stage manager, just slack? It was the 'Olivia' situation over again – and five doses of standing to be ready for action was enough to drive away sleep. It did not, but it was a fearful strain.

I received some good notices from the regional press for the Ellean part in '*Tanqueray*'. The *Manchester Courier* called me 'highly effective'; the *Newcastle Daily Chronicle* 'almost ideal'; the *Liverpool Daily Post* 'excellent', and the *Newcastle Daily Leader* flatteringly said they'd seen no better impersonation of the role.[3]

Nothing out of the way happened until we reached Glasgow. It was then that a rumour ran through the company that Her Majesty the Queen had ordered a command performance to be given before her at Balmoral.[4] But which of the plays had she chosen and who would be lucky enough to be in the cast? We felt sure it would not be the '*Tanqueray*'– it was a shrewd guess that it would be *The Idler* or *Liberty Hall*. I was not in the acting cast in the former, though was understudying the lead. So imagine my delight when it was confirmed that it was to be *Liberty Hall*. The Prince of Wales had clearly told his mother of this delightful play.

But the person who was almost delirious with joy and awe – equally mixed – was a dear little actor called Robson.[5] The men chaffed him mercilessly and frightened him out of his wits. This sort of thing:

---

[1] *The Triumph of the Philistines,* by Henry Arthur Jones (1895).

[2] In *The Second Mrs Tanqueray*, Ellean is the teenage daughter born to Aubrey Tanqueray and his first wife, who, abandoning her plan to become a nun, comes to live with her father and his second wife, Paula.

[3] These reviews have been pasted in to Dolan's manuscript.

[4] For a full account of this Royal Command performance, see Richard W. Schoch, *Queen Victoria and the Theatre of Her Age* (Basingstoke: Palgrave Macmillan, 2004), 84–7.

[5] E.M.Robson (1855–1932), English actor, son of Frederick Robson. He is also credited with being the writer, with William Lestocq, of a farce, *The Foundling*, which was premiered in New York in February 1895.

41

10. A new publicity portrait in 1895. **(V&A Images/Theatre Collections)**

'Now, mind, it is high treason to turn your back on the Queen.'

'Oh, as if I would! Oh, but I should love to play before Her Majesty.'

'You'll probably be presented, you know.'

'Presented? Shall I actually speak to Her Majesty?'

'Good Lord, no. That would be worse than turning your back on her.'

The acting manager went off to London to get replicas of the two chosen scenes painted to the scale of the tiny theatre in the ballroom at the castle. Only one week to do it in and get it delivered to Ballater.[6] Then there began the usual hitches. The Queen selected Saturday night. Now, command performances are not paid for by Royal patrons: the honour is enough. So the poor actor-manager has to pay all expenses; moreover Saturday, with its two performances, brings the largest returns. On presentation of the facts, the Queen graciously said that Monday would do. But that Monday was the bank holiday and worse than ever for the same reasons. GA was in despair.

I'm glad I wasn't the Acting Manager who had to settle it. Somehow he managed to get Her Majesty to make a great concession (not to be treated as a precedent). We would travel to Ballater on the Sabbath and play the same night. I had to get up betimes to hear Mass and just caught the train, for though it was a short journey we had to be on the spot as soon as possible to see everything was in order for the show.

We arrived at Ballater in a Scotch drizzle. Driven in wagonettes to the castle, we were peremptorily halted in a great courtyard where we could see, to our horror, all the theatrical baskets being unpacked in the rain. We were told the order had been given that none of them should be taken in to the castle because the last company that had given a command performance had carried away souvenirs! Imagine our fury and indignation with that company (which shall be nameless). I recalled Irving's words to me at Swinford Old Manor: 'Remember always to uphold the honour of the Profession.' The warning was evidently needed in some cases.

We were to be accommodated in the hotel at Ballater, but before going there, we were invited to be shown over the castle by Miss Knollys, chief Lady-in-Waiting to the Queen.[7] 'We' does not include the GAs, of course. I expect the Comptroller of the Household was giving them tea. The thing I chiefly remember are the carpets and the upholstery. Can you picture that, in each room you entered, you walked on and sat upon a different tartan of the various clans? (Edward VII made a clean sweep of all that.)

Miss Knollys was a perfectly charming chaperone and told us amusing stories. In 1887, the Golden Jubilee year, when the Indian princes were entertained at Balmoral, their religious principles forbade them from walking on certain 'sacred' colours. So the Rajahs skipped, zig-zag fashion, across the floor when received by Her Majesty to make their obeisances. Her Majesty congratulated herself afterwards: 'I was able to keep my countenance.'

Then we were photographed and GA must have joined us for I see he is in it. I have said a good deal about how smart we had to be in town. But in the country, on tour, we dropped all that. You may smile when you look at that picture to think that this is a group of actors and actresses from the renowned St James's Theatre.

---

[6] Town in Royal Deeside where Balmoral Castle is situated.

[7] Charlotte Knollys (1844–1930), later Lady of the Bedchamber and Private Secretary to Queen Alexandra, consort of Edward VII.

11. The St James's company at a photo call in the garden at Balmoral. George Alexander is in the middle row with Evelyn Millard on his right and Winifred Dolan on the end of the row (right). E M Robson is in the centre at the front. At the far right of the back row is Robert Shone, the Stage Manager. **(V&A Images/Theatre Collections)**

We then returned to the hotel at Ballater for a meal and a rest until it was time to return to the castle to dress for the performance.

Miss Granville[8] and I were sitting in the lounge when the Acting Manager came to us and said that the Queen expected everyone to attend divine service that evening in Crathie Church. He added a note from GA that this was a command and had to be treated as such: everyone *had* to go. Here was a quandary. Now, Miss Granville, though a Protestant, had been educated at a convent. She looked at me. 'Well, Dolan, what are you going to do?'

I said: 'I'm not going.'

'You must – it's a command.'

'You know well enough I can't go – there's a higher command I have to obey. I shall just lie as low as possible and hope they won't miss me.'

So they all went and I stayed where I was, but I couldn't help wondering and worrying about what the Dickens GA would say and do.

Back at the castle, we were shown into a number of small private rooms of the boudoir type in which to dress and make up. Miss Knollys told us the Queen herself had graciously gone round them to see everything necessary had been provided such as looking glasses and so on. She also warned us at this time not to expect applause. If the Queen thought fit, she would lead it herself. It did not sound exactly exhilarating and it was a gingerly business not to spill any powder or leave a grease mark on the inlaid tables. The Queen had not thought of that!

---

[8] An actress who had played Lady Plimdale in *Lady Windermere's Fan*, among other roles. She was always known in programmes and reviews as plain 'Miss Granville' – probably a stage name.

12. In 1894, the year before the St James's production at Balmoral, Tree's company had performed *The Ballad Monger* there, as depicted by the *Illustrated London News*. This was the ballroom stage that was 'so tiny that when we were all on it together, we were crowded like sheep in a fold.' **(Popperfoto/Getty Images)**

Just when we were ready, an official came round and, with profound apology, locked us in! The explanation for this extraordinary proceeding was that Her Majesty would be wheeled to the ballroom and was very sensitive about being seen in her chair – no chances were to be taken of peeping toms. When we went on to the stage, the duplicate scenery which had been painted in London had not yet properly dried and the smell of size was overpowering.[9] Moreover, the stage itself was so tiny that when we were all on it together, we were crowded like sheep in a fold.

Among the audience with the Queen were Princess Victoria, Prince Arthur, Princess Beatrice and her husband Prince Henry of Battenburg, the Duke and Duchess of York[10] and a number of favoured guests from the countryside.

Two powdered flunkeys six feet tall in the Royal livery – scarlet coat, plush breeches and oyster-coloured stockings – came and posted themselves at either edge of the curtain. GA promptly requested them to go away, but no, orders were orders. Half-way through the first Act, they disappeared – to reappear on each side of the stage with shovels of hot coals upon which they poured eau-de-cologne, thereby incensing the actors in more ways than one. The Royal nostrils had clearly not liked the smell of size. We were all soon coughing and choking, hardly able to get on with our words. GA looked as black as thunder but wore his Society smile.

---

[9] A glutinous solution used to seal a surface before painting or to stiffen fabric.
[10] Three of Queen Victoria's children: Princess Victoria (1840–1901); Prince Arthur, Duke of Connaught (1850–1942) and Princess Beatrice (1857–1944) and the Queen's grandson, the Duke of York, later King George V (1865–1936).

13. The programme for the Royal performance of R. C. Carton's *Liberty Hall* in 1895.
(V&A Images/Theatre Collections)

Quite soon we were treated to a little discreet applause, which quickly got out of hand and became quite human. That cheered us up. Between the acts, I asked one of the flunkeys to let me have a look at Her Majesty. He acquiesced, so I pulled the edge of the curtain very gently and had a peep. There she sat, the little mistress of an empire upon which (then) the sun never set. I said to the flunkey, my head half-way up to his shoulder: 'She's a wonderful old lady, isn't she?'

It must have been the use of the word 'old', for he looked at me and announced with great pomposity: 'There's nothing the matter with Her Majesty but her legs.'

When it was all over, the Queen was so delighted with us she sent word that the entire company without exception was to go to supper at which the Duke of York would preside. She was going to rest. So we all changed again into evening dress.

I went in to supper with an officer of the Guards. As he was in the 42nd Black Watch and an uncle of mine had been in the regiment and had been killed at Tel-El-Kebir, I thought it an opening for conversation.[11] He listened for a couple of minutes and then said: 'I say, if you want any supper, don't talk; they eat here like catching a train.' It was true. The gold plates were whisked away from the unwary while their forkful of mutton cutlet was on its way to their mouths. I am not exaggerating – the whole thing was over in twenty minutes! I suppose the Queen was waiting for us, because we were told we were all going to be presented.

---

[11] The decisive battle of the Urabi revolt in Egypt in 1882 when Britain acted to protect its interests in the region, including the Suez Canal.

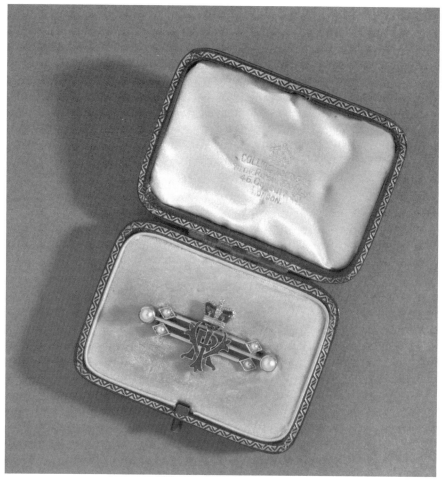

14. The brooch presented to Winifred Dolan by Queen Victoria.
(V&A Images/Theatre Collections)

We were assembled in a large room and one by one summoned into the presence. Of course, Mr and Mrs GA went first and were evidently engaged in conversation for there was an appreciable pause before Miss Millard was summoned. Then Sir Dighton Probyn popped in again and asked some questions.[12] They all pointed at me. I thought, that's it, they've discovered I didn't go to church, so I expect I'm out of it. The others – quite in the dark as I was – eyed me curiously and raised their eyebrows, but I shrugged an 'I don't know' and waited for events. After the other ladies had gone in, Sir Dighton came back and beckoned me. I rose and went in to make my curtsey.

The little Queen was standing between two enormously tall Indian aides-de-camp in gorgeous turbans and uniforms. All the guards were assembled in the

---

[12] General Sir Dighton Probyn (1833–1924), Comptroller of the Royal Household. Before that, a distinguished soldier and winner of the VC for his service in the Indian Mutiny of 1857-59.

background. The Queen's left hand rested on the Indian's arm and as I made my curtsey, with her right hand she slowly blew me three kisses with the sweetest smile. I could only look my thanks as I backed away.

After all the ladies came the men and first and foremost little Robson, flustered to the point of patriotic tears. The Queen spoke to him; she recalled her memory of the beautiful acting of his father and was glad to see his son at Balmoral. The dear man lost his head, forgot all warnings not to turn his back on the Queen and with clasped hands and three 'Oh your majestys' spiralled like a top in his effort to retire till someone caught him by the shoulders and landed him safely in the general crush. Her Majesty could again congratulate herself for 'keeping her countenance', but I could see she was hard put to it.

We had been a very great success and had, I hoped, done something to redeem the name of the profession. No other company had been so honoured. That night we slept at Ballater and the next morning we were off to open in Edinburgh. In due course, gifts arrived from Balmoral: for GA a cigarette box studded with diamonds; for Mrs GA a bracelet. The men got scarf pins with the royal monogram and the ladies brooches. When mine was handed to me, there was a note from Miss Knollys: the Queen wished it to be known she had specially selected the brooch for Miss Winifred Dolan.

A short while later, one of GA's assistants said to me: 'You didn't go to Crathie Church.'

'No,' I said, 'thank heaven they didn't miss me.'

'Oh, but they did. Her Majesty asked Mr Alexander if all the company had acceded to her wishes and he said "All but one who is a Roman Catholic and said it was against her conscience to do so." Don't you want to know what the Queen said?'

'What did she say?'

'She said, "And quite right too."'

Was that why she blew me three kisses? I wonder.

By the time we reached Edinburgh, Miss Millard was prostrated. The command performance on top of the strain of the tour had been too much for her. So I was called upon to take her place in the lead role of *The Triumph of the Philistines*.

GA very kindly came down just before curtain-up to run through the end of our love scene involving a rather complicated movement on my part in the embrace. I was nervous because, with eight parts in my mind, I was hazy about certain crosses – 'stage business' – in a play I had never seen from the front. When dear Lady Monckton came to wish me luck, I told her this. 'Never mind,' she said, 'I am on the stage in that scene and I'll give you the crosses.' She was of the old school in deportment and always stood, when she had nothing to do, with her hands elegantly placed together in front of her. Giving me the crosses was done by her thumb and I got through.

We had to be back in London in time to take part in a 'monster matinee' at the Lyceum which had been arranged in honour of Mrs Keeley's 90th birthday.[13] Granny Keeley was the doyenne of the profession and much beloved. Of course she

---

[13] Mary Anne Keeley (1805–1899), a veteran of the London stage, had celebrated her 90th birthday on 22 November 1895. She made her debut in London in the opera *Rosina* some seventy years before. She and her husband, Robert, managed the Lyceum from 1844 to 1847 and her last official public appearance was there in 1859. The public reception in 1895 was organised by the artist and writer, Walter Goodman, who had painted at least three portraits of Mrs Keeley and also wrote a biography, *The Keeleys on Stage and at Home* (London: Bentley and Son, 1895).

had retired long ago, but was linked with the great names of the past and in her time had herself been a star.

Scenes were played from all the current successes by their respective companies with additional attractions from solo contributors. We did Act III of *Liberty Hall*, so I was in it. It was a wonderful occasion – rows of royal patrons were listed on the programme while several minor ones were sitting in front. The Lyceum was packed (Irving and Ellen Terry were on tour in America and the theatre was sub-let).

When we had all done our piece there came the presentation to which the beneficiary was to reply. Mrs Keeley came to the stage, the prettiest, sweetest old lady, her figure and carriage still perfect and with lovely white hair. What a reception she got! When she replied in a few words, one heard a silver voice, unjarred by age, exquisitely modulated, every vowel and consonant falling like pearls on the ear, speaking no louder than in a drawing room, yet you knew it was being heard in the very last row of the gallery. Perfect! And for me personally, it was a joy to have played on the Lyceum stage just that once.

We had re-opened at the St James's with *Liberty Hall* and again, after a few nights and a very few hours' notice, I was told I was to take the lead role, as Miss Millard was once more prostrated by fatigue. This, of course, was my big chance: a leading part in London but – no press, no publicity. 'Olivia' over again. And I had never had one rehearsal. In London a new production is rehearsed for never less than six weeks; you have time to grow into a part, to mellow in it, to dovetail it with the other players.

Imagine a singer being given just the notes and words of a new song to learn with no score of the accompaniment and suddenly called upon to sing it for the first time with the accompanist she had never met and did not know her. This is no unfair analogy. Blanche Chilworth was a long part – throughout the four acts she is on stage all the time.

I confess, with shame, that I was unnerved – perhaps a little tired like Miss Millard – after ten weeks' tour with four other leading parts besides this one to carry in my head. I got through very creditably but I knew I was not at my best. I could not 'let myself go' because I was thinking about the words all the time.

I was very warmly received by a kind audience and we got the same number of curtain calls as ever after each act. But when it was over, as I was going up the stairs to my dressing room, I overheard Mrs GA's voice saying to someone she had brought backstage: 'What do you think of our new leading lady? Wasn't she splendid?' (dear Mrs GA!). Then came the answer in a man's cultivated voice: 'How beautiful, but my God, how cold!' Was he a drama critic? I never knew.

That GA had not said a word at curtain fall meant nothing. Neither had he wished me luck at the beginning: it was not his way. I never heard him commend anyone to their face: they might ask for a rise of salary! But if the gentleman repeated his verdict to GA, I could almost hear his shrug: 'Well, she's had her chance …'

If only I could have played it one night more after I'd got my second wind … But Miss Millard was back in the bill again and after we had played at Mrs Keeley's benefit on 27 November, I was once more out of a job. *The Prisoner of Zenda* went into rehearsal, there were only two women's parts in it, but not for me. Miss Millard made a hit in the role of Flavia – it fitted her like a glove. I have been blowing my own trumpet a good deal in this story so far, so it is only fair that I should now record this lowest of low points at the end of 1895 – out of work and with few prospects of a change of fortune.

Chapter VII

'Jog on, jog on, the footpath way'
– The Winter's Tale

It will be remembered that until I rejoined the St James's company for the Grand Tour in 1895, I had been absent from London for a whole year – on tour with Otho Stuart. During that year, many things happened which affected the stage world profoundly, so I will pause to touch on them now in retrospect.

There have been many scandals in the literary, artistic and social worlds, but none that caused such a sensation as that of Oscar Wilde. It was said of him that 'when he fell, he fell like Lucifer'. After bringing an unsuccessful action for criminal libel against the Marquis of Queensberry, he was himself arrested. The charge was heard at the Old Bailey where, on 25 May 1895, he was convicted and sentenced by Mr Justice Wills to two years' imprisonment with hard labour: the wretched man went to pick oakum in Reading Gaol.[1]

His struttings and posturings suited the period. He had become a cult among the epicene, a symbolic figure of that curious decade known as the 'Naughty Nineties'. Some three years later, he died in Paris where he had been living down at heel as Sebastian Melmoth and was buried in Bagneux cemetery. Nine years later, his remains were exhumed and reburied at Père Lachaise.

It was not surprising, then, that there arose a recrudescence of the moral crusade instigated by W. T. Stead of which I have already made mention. A Mrs Ormiston Chant now sprang into the limelight, demanding that the London County Council refuse the licence of the Empire Music Hall.[2] It was not the actual performances on the stage to which she objected, but the performances in the promenade which, she declared, were filled with loose women 'who glanced at men'. Mrs Ormiston Chant was also of the opinion that the lowering of lights when the curtain was up automatically lowered the moral calibre of such individuals (imagine playing to a lighted house!) Poor George Edwardes had to close the theatre until the matter was settled, throwing out of work the staff, performers, programme

---

[1] Wilde was arrested on 6 April 1895 and prosecuted for 'gross indecency' (under the Criminal Law Amendment Act passed in 1885 as mentioned above). He was found guilty after a second trial in May 1895, and sentenced to two years hard labour. After short stints in London gaols, he was transferred to Reading Gaol in November 1895.

[2] Laura Ormiston Chant (1848–1923), was an author, political activist and friend and confidante of George Bernard Shaw. Contrary to what Dolan writes, Mrs Ormiston Chant was concerned both with what went on in the promenade *and* on the stage of the Empire Theatre of Varieties, managed by George Edwardes. In evidence to the licensing committee in the summer of 1894, Mrs Ormiston Chant (and other members of the National Vigilance Society) opposed the Empire's re-licensing, claiming that 'the place at night is the habitual resort of prostitutes in pursuit of their traffic, and portions of the entertainment are most objectionable, obnoxious and against the best interests and moral well-being of the community at large.' After a lengthy hearing, the committee did grant an extension of the licence, but with the proviso that the promenade be closed and that intoxicating liquor be prohibited in the auditorium. Joseph W. Donohue, *Fantasies of Empire: The Empire Theatre of Varieties and the Licensing Controversy*, (University of Iowa Press, 2005), 97.

boys, call-boys, chuckers-out and all the rest of such folk involved in public entertainment.

In the end, the promenade was abolished. But the result was that the 'light ladies' transferred their 'glances at men' to Piccadilly, Regent Street and club-land. This then affected thousands of citizens who never went near the Empire where police supervision could – and did – ensure outward propriety.

But imagine the bombshell which exploded in the theatre world when Clement Scott picked up his pen in 1898 and wrote:

> It is really impossible for a woman to remain pure who adopts the stage as a profession. Everything is against her. The freedom of life, speech and gesture which is the rule behind the curtain render it almost impossible for a woman to preserve the simplicity of manner which is her greatest charm. Her whole life is artificial and unnatural to the last degree. Therefore it is an unhealthy life to live.[3]

Had the dear man gone mad?! The heads of the profession called for his dismissal from the *Daily Telegraph*; the rank and file practically demanded his head on a charger. As a matter of fact, Scott was ill and suffering from religious mania. The stage survived his attack on it but he, poor soul, did not. When it was realised he was old and ill and not responsible for his aberration, the profession gave him a benefit performance.[4] Two days later he was dead.

It is not to be denied that there was a sub-stratum of truth in all these charges levelled against the stage from various quarters, but they were emphatically not justified when applied to the 'legitimate' branch. Music halls were never exactly places of refinement in those days and the humour was Rabelaisian to say the least. Musical comedy, too, had the reputation of being conducted on doubtful lines. Admission behind the scenes of the *jeunesse dorée*[5] was calculated to lead to looseness of behaviour if not of morals. To be a chorus girl was to incur a black mark, and the growing habit of our peers marrying them outraged the British puritan's sense of fitness. But surely it must be to the credit of the said girls that so many of them withheld their favours unless and until accompanied by a wedding ring!

The truth is that at that time – halfway through the decade – a new era was developing. Ibsen and Shaw were breaking down barriers; no subject was taboo for dramatic exploitation; an epidemic of plays by new writers glorifying free love began to appear.[6] And where and by whom were these plays produced? In the crop

---

[3] Towards the end of 1897, Scott was asked by the evangelical periodical, *Great Thoughts*, if he would be interviewed by the editor on the subject of 'Does the theatre make for good?' The result, which was published in full in the January 1898 issue, was an attack on the morals of the stage in general and stage people in particular - especially actresses. In the furore that followed, Scott was dismissed from the *Daily Telegraph*, although he was subsequently re-hired. His reputation never recovered, however, and he retired to France in 1899 (*The Fall of Clement Scott*, Don Gillan [Copyright], www.stagebeauty.net).

[4] Along with Scott's reputation, his health and finances gradually deteriorated, and the benefit matinee for him took place some years later – on 23 June 1904 at His Majesty's, with Irving, Tree and Julia Neilson among those who performed. Scott saw little benefit from the money raised for him, however, because, as Dolan correctly recalls, he died only two days later after a long illness.

[5] Literally 'gilded youth' – young people of wealth and fashion.

[6] Dolan may have had in mind Netta Syrett's play, *The Finding of Nancy*, winner of the Playgoers' Club competition for new playwrights in 1901. Syrett's play concerned a young middle-class woman living an independent life in London, and maintaining an intimate relationship with a married man. See Katherine Newey, *Women's Theatre Writing in Victorian Britain* (Basingstoke: Palgrave Macmillan, 2005). In general terms, she is referring to what became known as the 'New Drama', influenced by Ibsen, and championed by George Bernard Shaw and William Archer, which included plays such as Shaw's *Mrs Warren's Profession*, and Elizabeth Robins and Florence Bell's *Alan's Wife*. However, Dolan's drawing together of immorality, the 'illegitimate' theatre, and Jewish involvement in new kinds of commercial structures in the theatre suggests the longevity of earlier, more stereotypically 'Victorian' values.

of new theatres whose names are familiar to us today. They were run by syndicates – all Jews – on strictly commercial lines. In time it proved the death knell for the actor-manager.[7]

So long as the old Queen lived, the trend was hardly noticeable, but with the Edwardian age it burst into full bloom. We see the mature fruit today in our divorce court lists, in the sex-appeal, striptease nudity of our cabaret entertainments, the hysterical worship of film stars.

To end this dissertation and hark back to 1895 on a happier note: in view of what I have written above, it is not without significance that on 25 May, Henry Irving's name appeared in the Birthday Honours List. He received a knighthood – the first ever bestowed on an actor. He had nothing to gain by his new title: his position as the acknowledged head of the theatrical profession was already assured and in accepting the knighthood he conferred upon the order more distinction than he received.[8]

It was, however, valued by him as an official recognition of his calling which – when music, painting, poetry, literature and sculpture were honoured freely – had long languished. Actresses could not be presented at court, and very few clubs – other than those connected with the theatre – offered membership to an actor.

Telegrams came from far and wide and Irving was presented with a congratulatory address signed by four thousand of all ranks of the profession from manager to scene-shifter.[9] On 18 July, he was summoned to Windsor and the Queen tapped him on the shoulder with a sword and commanded him to 'Arise, Sir Henry.' The new knight set a good example – his description on the playbills and programmes continued to be the familiar one of 'Henry Irving' (without even the Mr!).

Such were the conditions I would have to face in the future (though I did not know it at the time). I was out of a job at the very commencement of the winter season and too late to hope for a London engagement before the next spring. To whom could I turn for advice? To Ellen Terry – no, she was in the USA. To Clement Scott – I thought not. To Marion – she had been out of the bill, too, since she had left the St James's. I felt like throwing in the sponge.

Then a thought occurred: Cyril Maude had gone into management at the Haymarket; Bourchier, now married to Vi Vanbrugh, was managing at the Garrick and Boucicault, engaged to Irene Vanbrugh, was producing her at this theatre or the other.[10] They were all seasoned players who had had to branch out. Perhaps GA was

---

[7] Further discussion of this change in economic structures of the theatre industry can be found in Michael R. Booth, *Theatre in the Victorian Age* (Cambridge: Cambridge University Press, 1991), 55-7, and Tracy C. Davis, *The Economics of the British Stage 1800-1914* (Cambridge: Cambridge University Press, 2007) .

[8] By a cruel coincidence, the day that Irving's knighthood was announced, 25 May 1895, was the day Oscar Wilde was convicted at the Old Bailey of gross indecency. 'It was a salutary reminder of the taint of immorality which, for many people, still attached to the stage.' Jeffrey Richards, *Sir Henry Irving, A Victorian Actor and His World* (London: Hambledon and London, 2005), 109.

[9] The signatures were contained in a volume enclosed in a gold and crystal casket, designed by the actor and theatre manager, Johnston Forbes-Robertson. In returning thanks, Irving commented: 'In the olden times, our Britons showed their appreciation of a comrade by lifting him upon their shields and I cannot but feel, and feel it with unspeakable pride, that you, my brothers in our art, have lifted me on your shields.' Charles Hiatt, *Henry Irving: A Record and Review*, (London: George Bell and Sons, 1899).

[10] Cyril Maude (1862–1951), English stage and film actor and theatre manager. He shared in the management of the Haymarket from 1896 to 1905 and opened the Playhouse in London in 1907. Dion Boucicault Jr (1859–1929), American-born actor and stage director, the son of a well-known actor and dramatist of the same name. He and Irene Vanbrugh spent several successful years in Australia before returning to London in 1896. They married in 1901. Among his other achievements, Boucicault directed the first performance of J.M. Barrie's *Peter Pan* in London at the end of 1904, with his sister, Nina, in the title role.

not displeased with me after all – I was simply a victim of the system like all the rest.

Just as I was plucking up hope, who should walk into my digs one day in 1896 but Alfred Austin. He had just been made Poet Laureate to an outcry in the literary world.[11] He had come to persuade me to leave the stage – no life for a lady and so on. 'Of course, if you were a success, I should be very proud of you. But it does not suit me that my niece should be playing insignificant parts in London.'

I told him what parts I had played and that my salary had been £5 a week (that is, with two matinees). He gasped. Then he said: 'I've just seen George Alexander and he tells me you will never do any good.' He rose to go and, as a parting shot, said: 'I hope you will never use my name.' I was so angry I told him it would do me no good as he was not very popular. He smiled his ineffable smile and replied: 'No, I always hit out from the shoulder and they don't like that!' And with that he was gone.

When I told my parents, they were furious and wrote to Uncle Alfred to say that he must never interfere again. Next morning I presented myself at the GAs' home and caught them at breakfast. I told GA what my uncle had said. He looked at his wife and then at me.

'Did you say that?' I asked.

'Certainly not,' he replied. 'I told him I did not think you would ever be a leading lady, but that I was very pleased with your work and you should win a good position for yourself in time.'

He told me he would always give me parts when he could and that he liked to have me in the theatre because if his leading man fell down the stairs, he knew I would put on his clothes and pull the piece through! So with laughter on both sides I went away determined to stick it out. Meanwhile, I would go home for a short holiday and then run over to Paris to see what I could learn from the French stage. I had a great friend ten years older than myself who had lived in France and who said she would go with me. It was my first visit to Paris and I missed nothing one ought to see with such a friend as a guide. Of course we did the rounds of the main theatres and the highlight for me were Jane Hading, a beautiful creature, with Guitry, a superb actor, in *Les Amants*; Coquelin in *Cyrano de Bergerac* – unsurpassable - and a de Musset play at the Comedie-Française – such finished acting as I had never dreamed of![12]

Thénard of the Comedie had recited at one of Aunt Mary's parties and I had been introduced to her.[13] So I wrote and asked if I might call. She sent me a card for her classes and I attended, although I didn't learn much: the pupils were very young, rich demoiselles whom she taught to recite innocuous poems. I also rubbed up my French at one of the institutes, for though I could read and understand, I could hardly speak the language at all.

While I was in Paris, I was surprised to receive a letter from GA. He asked me to find out who owned the rights to a play called *Le Prince d'Aurec* done last at

---

[11] It was said that Austin became Poet Laureate – four years after Tennyson's death - almost by default in that there was no other suitable candidate. His critics attacked him as snobbish, tasteless and with limited poetic talent.
[12] The Comédie-Française is France's state theatre, dating back to 1680. Jane Hading (1859–1933), leading French actress. Lucien Germain Guitry (1860–1925), French actor, and father of the leading Parisian actor, Sacha Guitry. Benoit-Constant Coquelin (1841–1909), French actor. *Cyrano de Bergerac* by Edmond Rostand (1897). Alfred Louis Charles de Musset (1810–1857), French dramatist, poet and novelist.
[13] Jenny Thénard (1847–1920), a leading actress at the Comédie-Française between 1876 and 1884 and subsequently a teacher of speech and drama.

the Gymnase with Hading in it.[14] I was not to make it known that I was his 'ambassador', but was to discover how much he would have to pay for the English-speaking rights. An ambassador! Gracious me! What next?

---

[14] *Le Prince d'Aurec* by Henri Lavedan. This satire on the nobility, with its overtones of anti-Semitism, was apparently originally offered by Lavedan to the Comédie-Française, but was thought 'too startling, too bold to suit the tastes and favour of a certain majority of the public'. (*New York Times*, 19 June 1892). It did, however, find a home at the Vaudeville in 1892 with Hading in the cast. This production was, presumably, in the original French if Alexander was seeking the English-speaking rights. The *New York Times* reported the following year that a translated version was being prepared for an American stock company, but it is not clear whether this ever went ahead.

Chapter VIII

'Fortune brings in some boats that are not steer'd'
– Cymbeline

When I returned to England, I found a letter awaiting me from GA. It asked me to come to see him at once as he had a proposal.

Next morning I presented myself at his office in the theatre and he told me he was going to put on *As You Like It* when '*Zenda*' came off, with Julia Neilson to play Rosalind.[1] But he couldn't get her without Fred Terry, her husband. There was no role for Fred, of course, so as part of the £100 a week deal for the two of them, he would take the Royalty Theatre and put on a farcical comedy with Fred in the lead.

Now, at this time, GA's assistant was a man called Legge.[2] 'Legge's got it into his head he wants to be an acting manager,' said GA. 'I've told him it's not in him, but to convince him I'm going to give him a trial at the Royalty. Would you like to take his place as my secretary on the understanding that if and when I give up the Royalty you have kept his seat warm for him to come back to?'

I accepted. It got me a footing again at the St James's, there was no knowing what it might lead to and it meant no more financial worry for at least some months ahead. I was broke – all my savings had gone. I started my duties there and then and I'll describe a typical timetable as experience evolved it.

First I had to be at two theatres for the morning's letters and take them to Pont Street by nine o'clock[3] – this meant my day started at about 8am. I only left my position for a quick lunch at some restaurant (tea at the office) and left it around 6 or 6.30pm. Home to dinner. Back at 7.30pm and on duty until close to midnight. This was how it was except on Sundays for six months – pretty strenuous.

My duties included: taking instructions concerning the letters and answering them; keeping GA posted as to his various engagements; writing his speeches when he was called upon to make them; interviewing endless people on various matters and distributing the pay envelopes at the Royalty on Friday nights. One day GA asked me to take over the box office in the lunch hour and I jumped at that. He was certainly giving me opportunities that no woman had had at that time.

In addition to all that, I was his reader of plays. This required me to keep abreast of a pile of scripts never less than two feet high. On my own responsibility,

---

[1] Julia Neilson (1868–1957), English actress. In 1890, she married Fred Terry (1863–1933), English actor and younger brother of Ellen Terry.

[2] R.G. Legge (b.1864), assistant and general factotum to George Alexander. The title 'acting manager' was in general use in the English theatre until about 1910. It meant a business administrator who, in essence, was the actor-manager's right-hand man on the production side. Arguably the most celebrated was Bram Stoker, known chiefly now as the author of *Dracula*. He was acting manager and personal assistant to Irving at the Lyceum for some 27 years.

[3] Number 57, Pont Street – the Alexanders' fashionable home in Knightsbridge, London, to which they moved from Park Row in 1895. Lillie Langtry was a near neighbour for a time.

I could reject each play or, if I were in doubt as to a 'possible', submit a scenario of it, upon which GA would decide whether to read it.

That pile never grew smaller – all the world was apparently writing plays: clerks, bricklayers, maiden aunts … people without a glimmer of stage craft; others who could write good dialogue but with impossible plots, or good ideas they could not clothe in dialogue. For reasons I will tell you later, I read every one of them for fear a gem lay hidden in the trash.

I only found one, but it was reward enough. It was not typed and the writer's script was all but indecipherable. I was about to give it up when I glanced again at the author's name. I recognised him as someone who'd married a girl in the company and I knew they were hard up. So I went at it again: it was a lovely little one-act play. I took it to GA and told him who it was by and left it with him. He returned, saying: 'Tell the fellow to type it – I'm not going to puzzle through a thing like that.'

I typed it – it only took an hour – and presented it to GA the same night. He said: 'He can't have … did you type it?' I said yes, it was worth it. He gave me a look that shouted 'you little fool', but he bought it for £40. On another occasion, one would-be playwright enclosed a letter with his play along these lines: 'I am a plain working man but a genius. I want £1,000 for my play or £100 down on account and £25 per week for royalties.' Unfortunately, his play did not have the mark of genius about it.

The comedy that GA had found for Fred Terry at the Royalty was *His Little Dodge*.[4] It was a farce adapted from the French. I could tell it had been heavily edited, in fact so emasculated that it lacked the punch all farces must have. When we opened the papers after the first performance, the less reputable of them raised the old crusade cry again and Jerome K. Jerome wrote a libellous article declaring that drunken club-men had lounged in the stalls and that the women were worse for drink.[5] All the suggestive passages in the French original were quoted as having been present in the play and so on.

When I got to the office, GA, Legge and the investment agent of Lord Rothschild, who was backing the venture, were assembled in consternation. The only explanation that GA could offer for Jerome's attack on him was that he had rejected all the man's plays. He refused to bring a libel action, saying 'It is beneath contempt and I take my stand on my public character. The Box Office must give the verdict.' How strong and how wise. The Box Office did vindicate him and the piece prospered.

The impresario Ben Greet bought the touring rights to *His Little Dodge* and GA asked Legge to produce the play for him as he couldn't spare anyone from the St James's.[6] 'It'll be £25 in your pocket.' I must explain that on touring bills, they

---

[4] *His Little Dodge* (1896), adapted by Justin Huntly McCarthy from the French farce *Le Système Ribadier* by George Feydeau and Maurice Hennequin.
[5] Jerome K. Jerome (1859–1927) was the author of *Three Men in a Boat* among other works. In 1893, he started his own two-penny weekly magazine, *Today*, and the offending article about *His Little Dodge* probably appeared within its pages. Although Alexander declined to bring a court action, Jerome's perilous style of journalism brought one the following year (1897). A businessman, Samson Fox, sued him and the magazine over a perceived libel. Fox won only a token one farthing in damages, but Jerome's costs of £9,000 were ruinous. He had to sell his interest in *Today* and in a satirical magazine he co-edited, *The Idler*. Jerome wrote of the saga: 'I have the satisfaction of boasting that it was the longest case, and one of the most expensive, ever heard in the Court of Queen's Bench.'
[6] Sir Philip Barling 'Ben' Greet (1857–1936), English actor, director and impresario. After a spell as a schoolmaster, Greet made his professional debut in 1883 and three years later began touring with his own company, principally performing in schools and in the open air. Shakespeare was presented in the original text in simplified productions. He toured North America with his Elizabethan Stage Society of England from 1902–14 and became Director of the Old Vic

write 'From the XXX Theatre, London' and this means the company has been rehearsed by that theatre's stage manager. It looks well.

Poor Legge threw up his hands in dismay. He had never seen a rehearsal, he didn't know the business and so on. 'But good God, man,' GA cried, exasperated, 'you've seen it every night from the front! Winifred, you go, I bet you know every touch.' Well of course I did, so I went.

Dear old Ben Greet nearly had a fit when I told him I had come to produce *His Little Dodge* for the tour. But, but … I wasn't a *man* (none available). But it must be a *man* (very sorry etc). The company will never submit to (he checked the insult on his tongue). He went on: 'A *man*. It must be a *man*, do you hear?' I said that Mr Alexander would not have sent me if he had not been confident that I … He stopped me short. 'My dear lady, you don't understand. A *man* is necessary to open at Kilburn, hold the book, work the curtain – and besides, the scene-shifters would never obey you. Oh dear, oh dear.'

He was almost in tears and I felt sorry for him – it was such a risk in his eyes. 'Come now, Mr Greet,' I said, 'give me my chance and I'll do it for a fiver.' I said this because I wanted so much to prove I could do it.

'All right,' he sighed, 'but I shall have to attend every rehearsal and I am so busy with my other companies. Fire away then!'

He summoned the company on to the stage and apologised for me! I must say they looked pretty chilly. So with a 'we must make the best of it', he bade me start. And who do you think was the leading lady? Cora Stuart – 'Lavender' on whose blotter I had written my name in the Grand Theatre, Leeds, in 1887![7] We started rehearsal and at the end of an hour, Greet rose from his chair and looked at me in silence, then said in awed tones: 'God bless my soul, I've never seen such a thing in my life!' and walked out. I never saw him again until years later when we met at Ellen Terry's funeral. I got my fiver and proved a woman could do some jobs as well as a man.

It had been a joy to coach true professionals. No spade-work to do – every point taken. Cora Stuart wrote me a lovely letter afterwards – too flattering to reproduce here. We did the show at Kilburn without a hitch and the scene-shifters enjoyed the joke as much as I did. It was typical that GA never asked me how I had got on and I held my tongue about the fiver. He would never have understood that.

Towards the end of 1896, Mr and Mrs GA came into the office at St James's en route to somewhere. He sat down and said casually: 'I want you to run over to Paris for me, Coquelin is doing a play that I'm told has a good part for me. Go and see it, wire your opinion and I will write and tell you what to do. That all right?' 'Rather!'

At this point, Mrs GA asked if she might go too. GA agreed, on condition that I did not seek or take her advice. I was secretly relieved that I was not going alone.

---

in 1914. 'Greet's arduous and little publicised labours for Shakespearean production were splendidly rewarded during the war years when he and his company were invited to raise the Shakespearean banner at the Old Vic, and kept it flying there while the actor-managers were striking their flags on all sides.' George Rowell, *The Victorian Theatre 1792–1914* (Second Edition, Cambridge: Cambridge University Press, 1978), 141.
[7] Cora Stuart (1857–1940), was an English actress, who at the time of this tour of *His Little Dodge*, was making her name more as a musical comedy performer. One of her most popular pieces was E. Haslingden Russell's one-act sketch, *The Fair Equestrienne* or, *The Circus Rider*. To an interviewer in 1894, Miss Stuart said: 'Well, I suppose you have come to blow me up for deserting the theatres for the halls?' 'Nothing of the kind, Miss Stuart,' replied the interviewer. 'I should indeed be unreasonable to complain of your behaviour. It may be a loss to the theatre, but, at the same time, sketch artists who can act are by no means so plentiful that we can afford to blow them up when we have them.' (*On and Off*, Judy's Annual, London, 1894, p.38, courtesy of John Culme's *Footlight Notes*.)

So off we went. First class, Grand Hotel and all the rest of it. That previous trip to Paris stood me in good stead now. I showed Mrs GA round all the right shops and at the Maison de Blanc she must have spent £200 at least.[8] It was fun.

That night we went to see Coquelin's play. For two acts, we were both delighted. Act III? No. Off! Mrs GA got really vexed with me. I stuck to my opinion but said that, instead of giving a negative, I would write to GA and offer my reasons. 'Then I shall write and tell him it is the very part for him,' she replied.

'Yes, do,' I said, 'he should hear both sides,' (I felt it better to be politic with her), 'but my point is that the play won't suit the St James's.' So we both wrote and peace was restored.

We had another day's sightseeing and at night went to see Bernhardt in a play by de Musset called *Lorenzaccio*.[9] Here, I thought, was the very thing for GA, but Mrs GA did not care for it. The fact was it suffered from Sarah B playing a male part - the English public never appreciated tours de force. GA wired that he was coming over and I was to get seats again for Coquelin's play.

At the end of Act II he turned to me and said: 'I thought you had better judgement than to turn this down.' I said, 'Wait a bit.' Half-way through Act III, I heard him muttering 'This is no good' and as the curtain fell, he rose. 'Come on, this is no use to me. Let's go and speak to Coquelin.' So we went behind to his dressing room and had a chat. Coquelin said: 'I could have told you, *mon cher*, it would not do for you. The part, yes, the play …' He shrugged.

When I told GA about *Lorenzaccio* he said he would stay another night to see it. He bought it. We went behind to Bernhardt's dressing room and she asked Mrs GA and myself to tea at her house in Rue Pereire next day. GA went home, but was so pleased he gave us a further week's holiday in Paris. We went to Bernhardt's home and were shown into a large room with a great divan on a raised platform and a canopy over it. A *major-domo* solemnly ushered in the Divine Sarah, who sat on her throne while she dispensed hospitality. She was charming - but did not unbend as she had to GA! It was an interesting experience anyhow.

Back in London, the run of *The Prisoner of Zenda* had closed and thus Miss Millard's engagement had come to an end. In spite of her amazing success as Flavia, she never got another important part and, a short while later, married and left the stage. Julia Neilson was now our leading lady and a new recruit was a very charming American girl called Fay Davis, who stayed with us for two years.[10] She played Celia in *As You Like It* which was now put into rehearsal.

GA sent me to the British Museum to read up all I could find as to how Macready had produced the play.[11] That was my first introduction to the Reading

---

[8] Probably La Grande Maison de Blanc, a fashionable department store on Place de l'Opéra, founded in 1863 and particularly known for its lingerie.

[9] *Lorenzaccio* by Alfred de Musset. De Musset was 23 when he started *Lorenzaccio* during a celebrated love affair with the writer George Sand. It was Sand who inspired Musset to write the play by giving him a copy of her playlet *Une Conspiration en 1537*. Still stinging from the public failure of his first play, de Musset wrote *Lorenzaccio* as a bit of *'theatre dans un fauteuil'* – armchair theatre that was simply designed to be read as literature and not performed. It was not until 1896, when Bernhardt brought the role of Lorenzo to the stage, that the play was first produced. This was more than 60 years after it had been written and almost forty years after de Musset's death in 1857. Bernhardt brought the play to the Adelphi in 1897. *Curtain Up*, the Internet Theatre Magazine (www.curtainup.com).

[10] Fay Davis (1872–1945), was born in Boston, Massachusetts and came to England in 1895 to join Sir Charles Wyndham's company, from where she went on to the St James's. She stayed there for five years, returning to the United States in 1902. Back in England in 1906, she appeared in many leading Shakespearean roles. ' (…) an actress who could make us smile by her pleasant humour, command our tears by her gentle and natural pathos, and interest us always by the freshness of her style and the earnestness and attraction of her methods.' Boyle Lawrence (ed.), *Celebrities of the Stage*, (London: George Newnes, 1900), 87.

Room, which I found of good use to me later on. I had to be at GA's elbow at every rehearsal and make up for the lost time on my other duties as best I could.

At night I had to be at the Royalty to keep an eye on Legge, report on the players and keep a rather recalcitrant conductor of the orchestra up to the mark. He would play short pieces, break off and begin again, a fault that enraged GA. In truth it was really Legge's business to do all this. When the last act started, I had to hurry back to the St James's for the last postal delivery and receive instructions for the following day. I never got home before 12.30am, but it was intensely interesting and I learned about running a theatre from the office rather than the stage.

Kate Phillips played Audrey in *As You Like It* – a small part for a star 'pro'.[12] She got a better engagement and GA released her. I stepped into the part for the run and the Grand Tour of 1897. Again, no notices, no publicity. Ehem! It was a beautiful production scenically and Julia Neilson a brave Rosalind, although in my opinion there was too much of the principal boy about it.[13] The Bard was not really GA's forte. It only ran for four months (December 1896–March 1897), so after the tour (another two months), I was out again. The Royalty was closed and Legge returned to the seat I had kept warm for him.

'Resting' is the profession's euphemism for being out of work. My capital had long ago vanished and as my wardrobe gave out, it had to be replenished. At that time, £4–5 a week had to cover not just a room and food, but also what I will lump together as raiment, doctor's bills, travel and the incidentals that were forever cropping up. It was impossible to save enough for rainy days if they lasted months. How did I manage to hold out? By 'side-shows', I might call them: engagements to produce London plays for an excellent amateur dramatic society in Glasgow, £25 a time; playing lead in amateur shows as the only 'pro', eg at Shrewsbury in Lord Kilmorey's Shropshire Yeomanry Centenary Pageant; journalism, short stories and lyrics for a song-writer; commissions to supply text for illustrations – for instance, on one occasion it was Japanese costumes, which meant research work at the British Museum's Reading Room.

Once I was even a drama critic for a while. An editor who liked my work asked me to deputise for the paper's own critic, who had been ordered abroad after a severe illness. During that time, Bourchier produced John Oliver Hobbes' play, *The Bishop's Move*.[14] Bourchier's Catholic Bishop was very true to life and the play brilliant. I gave them both a very good notice and a day or two later, I came across sandwich-board men in the Strand with my notice on their boards, coupled with one from *The Times*. Of course mine was not 'signed' – I was an understudy, no publicity again. Ehem!

---

[11] William Charles Macready (1793–1873), was actor-manager of Covent Garden (1837–39) and Drury Lane (1841–43) and staged *As You Like It* at both. 'He had a strong sense of a production's unity and coherence, used large numbers of actors intelligently and paid a great deal of attention to scenic harmony and scenic illustration of a text.' Michael R. Booth, *Theatre in the Victorian Age*, (Cambridge: Cambridge University Press, 1991), 42.

[12] Kate Phillips (1856–1931), English actress who worked with the Kendals and Irving, and was, according to W. Macqueen-Pope, the daughter of Philip Goldney, a 'fox-hunting squire'. *St James's: Theatre of Distinction* (London, W.H. Allen, 1958), 73.

[13] A reference to the pantomime tradition – at its height in the late-Victorian era – of a young woman, invariably in short tunic and long boots, playing the romantic male hero. In the early days of pantomime, when women wore long dresses, the principal boy's outfit attracted a large male audience. Elizabeth Poole, who played such parts in the 1830s, is credited with introducing the further tradition of the slapped thigh. (History of Pantomime, www.SheffieldTheatres.co.uk).

[14] John Oliver Hobbes, pen-name for Pearl Mary-Teresa Richards Craigie (1867–1906), American author and playwright, active in Europe. *The Bishop's Move*, a comedy of manners by Hobbes and Murray Carson, presented at the Garrick Theatre in 1902.

Also, GA told Mr Vincent, now Stage Manager at the St James's, to give me the typing of all prompt copies.[15] The fellow took it upon himself to say he wanted them as quickly as a typing office would do them (though there, each act was handed out to different clerks). Thus it meant that, at the end of a day's work such as I have described, I would be sitting up until 4am to get it done. But it paid well and I was glad to have it to do.

Yes, 'resting' is hard work and sometimes means an oasis of no work at all. I nearly touched bottom once. I could only get a morning job as secretary to an old lady novelist – 15 shillings a week. I lived on it for three weeks and went hungry.

---

[15] H. H. Vincent (1848–1913), English actor, stalwart of the St James's company, who served as stage manager between 1892 and 1900.

Chapter IX

'Tis a very excellent piece of work, madam lady ...'
– The Taming of the Shrew

There is another side of my stage life I have not mentioned; some of it took place in the years I have already recorded, some much later – well into the twentieth century – and I now tell of it under a section by itself. It harks back to something I first did when I was just eight years old. Remember *Rosabella*?

If acting is a gamble, play-writing is worse. Success is not won solely by good work, and on top of that, any success won must be sustained by good, if not better, work. In the first place, a play must be read (remember the pile two feet high) which generally means it is kept for three or four months – precious time lost if the play is at all topical. A reminder brings it back unread and refused.

Then it must fit the manager as actor and manager, that is, suit his policy at that particular moment ('I can't do another play like this so soon. Send it back, say I like it, but regret ...'). If it has been made to measure for a certain man, it will be useless for any other not of the same type.

Then circumstances may intervene: for instance, a sudden vote of censure in the House of Commons might bring a general election, which can postpone productions. A play postponed seldom gets another chance – the waters close up. Some of the greatest successes seemed fore-doomed to failure. It was ten years before Somerset Maugham had a play accepted.[1] *The Scarlet Pimpernel* was considered a dud on production – it made Fred Terry's fortune.[2] Mrs Kendal once told me she never forgave herself for refusing *Jim The Penman* – it graced the stage, on and off, for twenty years.[3] Bourchier took Sutro's *The Walls of Jericho* as a stop-gap – it ran for three years.[4] I could go on.

Early on in my career I thought I'd try my hand, beginning with an adaptation – a sure card to start with. To keep up my French, I used to read French

---

[1] W. Somerset Maugham (1874–1965), British novelist and playwright. It took, in fact, only five years for Maugham's first full-length play, *A Man of Honour*, to be produced. He wrote it in 1898 – a year after his first novel was published – and it was presented by the Stage Society at the Imperial Theatre, London in February 1903 (two performances) and at the Avenue Theatre, London in February 1904 (28 performances). Anthony Curtis and John Whitehead (eds.), *W. Somerset Maugham: the Critical Heritage,*(London: Routledge & Kegan Paul, 1987), 59.

[2] *The Scarlet Pimpernel* by Baroness Emmuska Orczy was first performed at the Theatre Royal in Nottingham in October 1903 before the novel had been published. It was unsuccessful, but Fred Terry had confidence in the play and, with a re-written last act, he took it to London where it opened at the New Theatre on 5 January 1905. Although the critics branded it old-fashioned, the play became a favourite with London audiences and played more than 2,000 performances.

[3] *Jim the Penman* by Charles Young (Haymarket, April 1886). Allardyce Nicoll argues that this play is 'a purposeful melodrama not unworthy to stand beside Taylor's *The Ticket-of-Leave Man*, and Jones's *The Silver King.*' *A History of English Drama, 1660-1900*, Vol. V, *Late Nineteenth Century Drama, 1850-1900* (Cambridge: Cambridge University Press, 1959), 150.

[4] *The Walls of Jericho* by Alfred Sutro (1904).

books and was struck by the dramatic possibilities of Dumas' *Une Fille Du Regent*.[5] I adapted it and asked GA to read it. He promised and in due course called me and said he was trying to book an American tour and if he went, he would do my play. He didn't go. There was, at that time, a glut of costume plays on in London, including *The Three Musketeers* being played by two houses against each other.[6] GA was justified in not competing. So my play never saw the light.

Next, I dramatised another novel, *Serge Panine*, and sent it to Mrs Kendal.[7] She replied that she'd read it with pleasure and that it was full of good characters. The heroine was delightful, but too young for her to attempt.

I came across a volume of contes by Theophile Gautier and hit on one entitled *Avatar*.[8] This I made into a four-act play and called it *Octave's Eyes*. I asked GA to read it. 'Come and read it yourself at Pont Street,' he said. It was a great favour, but what an ordeal. I got through it, Mr and Mrs GA seated side by side on a settee, silent throughout the two hours it took. When I finished, GA said: 'Ring the bell for a cab, we'll go down to the theatre. I accept your wonderful play and we'll get a contract signed at once.' I could not believe my ears.

As we drove up to the theatre, an agitated acting manager rushed out to say that Sir-somebody-or-other had been waiting for an hour. 'Good Lord,' cried GA, 'you put everything out of my head, Winifred. Trot along. See you tonight.' For a week he avoided me, I couldn't catch him. Eventually he returned the script saying he'd given it to someone else to read and had been advised not to risk it.

That play went round London. I got encomiums but nothing else. I sent it to Daniel Frohman, the leading impresario in America.[9] He returned it with a letter which said: 'With personal regret. It is the best play that has come into my hands for a long time. But all my plays are read by a committee of seven gentlemen and they have reluctantly turned it down.'

A month later, he wrote again. 'May I have the play back for consideration? I will pay all expenses.' It came back again. Then one of the seven gentlemen wrote to ask if *he* might have it to try to place with another management. He kept it for six months, but returned it with some tart remarks about people 'who played safe'.

I wrote *The Showman* and read it to GA. This was my first original play, and his verdict was that if he could put Jones's or Pinero's name to it, he would produce it the next day. But it wasn't strong enough to run for more than 100 performances and he never accepted a play that he did not hope and expect would carry two seasons. Try Hawtrey, he said.[10]

---

[5] *Une Fille du Regent* by Alexandre Dumas père (1845), a romance in four volumes. Winifred Dolan was presumably unaware that a dramatised English language adaptation had been published in the United States many years before her idea. *The Regent's Daughter* 'a serio-comic play in five acts' by William Young, (New York: D. Appleton, 1854). There is no record of its ever having been performed.

[6] *The Three Musketeers*, based on the novel by Alexandre Dumas père (1844). The competing productions referred to are thought to be the adaptations – one by Henry Hamilton and the other by Sydney Grundy – staged in 1898 at the Globe and Her Majesty's. Erroll Sherson, *London's Lost Theatres of the Nineteenth Century,* (London: The Bodley Head, 1925), 251.

[7] *Serge Panine* by George Ohnet (1881). This novel was not well received by the critics, but became extremely popular with the French public and has gone through 150 French editions. A dramatised version was presented in Paris in 1884 and there were two films.

[8] Theophile Gautier (1811–1872), French poet, dramatist and novelist, known for his short stories or novellas.

[9] Daniel Frohman (1851–1940), was an influential American theatre manager, who ran various companies in the United States, notably the New Lyceum. He developed a system of sending a production out on the road while also keeping it in New York. He later became involved in the film industry and was a producer with Adolph Zukor in the Famous Players Film Company. Autobiographical works include *Memories of a Manager* (Heinemann, 1911), and *Daniel Frohman Presents: an Autobiography*, (Kendall, 1935).

[10] Charles Henry Hawtrey (1858–1923), English actor and producer/manager.

Mr Hawtrey sent for me and in his office were three or four men. One came forward and said: 'I am Mr Hawtrey's reader, I think very highly of your play and want him to do it. He will see you in a few minutes.'

As he spoke, a door opened and Hawtrey beckoned to me. As I entered, he hurled a forefinger at me and said in a burst: 'Did you write that play yourself?'

'Of course I did.'

'Unaided?'

'Yes.'

'Damn. I've just lost £5. I bet no woman could have written it.'

He explained that he wanted to do it but on condition that he married the girl in the end. 'I must, the public expect it.' Now, without going through the whole plot, suffice to say that it would have been preposterous for Hawtrey's character to have married the girl. He rose. 'Take it or leave it.' Perhaps I was swollen-headed. I left it.

I wrote *The Lion Cub* and read it to GA. 'Your characterisation is perfect, but there's not enough grip in your plot for a long run. Persevere, it'll come.' It went the rounds and at last Ian Robertson and his manager sent for me.[11] He was very patronising. 'So you write plays, do you, Miss Dolan?'

'I try to' (with a bewitching smile).

'Quite. Now this play of yours would suit us nicely with a little alteration. There is no necessity for the first act and the play would gain by cutting it out.' (Also saving expense!)

I saw the point at once and said: 'I agree. Give me back the script.'

He did so. 'Yes, read it over and come and see me again.'

That night I cut out the act, inserted the extra lines in Act II to elucidate the situation and presented myself at the theatre. 'You've done it?'

'Yes, you were quite right. Thank you for pointing it out to me.'

'Well! If you think you can do a difficult thing like that without experience' – and he handed me back the play. 'Good morning.'

Later on, I tumbled to it. I should have asked him kindly to teach me how to write. What a little fool. Of course the man wanted to do it himself and claim half the authorship and royalties! Nobody else made me an offer for the play. I would never make a good businesswoman.

I went back to adaptation. I found a clever German story, the writer long dead so no bother with copyright. It was a delicious comedy set in an enclave on the continent, which I called Puppenthum, with a petty prince and a ridiculous court. I called it *In Spite of Himself* and at last it reached Dennis Eadie at the Royalty, a tiny theatre in Soho just fitted for such a piece.[12] He sent for me. 'I'm sorry to tell you I can't do the play. I'm longing to play the part, but my partner, Vedrenne, won't have it.' So he handed me back the script.

A year or so later, Vedrenne died. I asked Eadie if he'd take it now. 'Yes,' he said, 'but I can't do it this year.' His appearance shocked me. Six months later he died too.[13]

---

[11] Probably Ian Forbes-Robertson, English actor-manager.

[12] Dennis Eadie (1875–1928), co-manager of the Royalty Theatre, London, from 1911 with J.E.(John Eugene) Vedrenne (1867–1930). Their aim at the newly-refurbished Royalty was to establish a home for contemporary, but commercially viable, drama. 'In an informal statement of purpose, issued during their third season, both talked of staging experimental works of artistic merit.' Joel H Kaplan and Sheila Stowell, *Theatre and Fashion: Oscar Wilde to the Suffragettes*, (Cambridge: Cambridge University Press, 1994), 140.

[13] As far as this particular episode is concerned, Dolan's memory seems to have failed her. Dennis Eadie died first – on 10 June 1928. Vedrenne's death is recorded as 12 February 1930.

I was introduced to George Power, an Irishman with a lovely brogue.[14] He was a singer of some note and wanted me to write 'an Irish sketch' for two people to perform at music-hall. I wrote *A Man Of His Word* for a gentleman and a valet who fulfilled, literally, all his orders. When told to air his master's dress clothes, he wore them, and so on. George was delighted. I received £25 and he got a week's engagement at Margate.

After the first performance, he wired me: 'Went like fire – booked seven weeks' tour.' At last, I thought. But before the week was out, George got a cable from his brother, Tyrone Power, in New York. Tyrone had wrecked a fine career with drink, married a girl who saved him from the curse and was doing well. Alas, she had just died on the operating table. The cable ran: 'For God's sake come to me or I will go to the dogs again. Engagement waiting you here – $20 a week.' George cancelled his tour and went. My sketch was never played again.

Then I wrote, with a musician friend, a sketch called *The Little Tin God* – about an admiring widow and an opera tenor who in private life can only stutter. When he tries to talk, the widow can only cry agonisingly 'Sing it, sing it!' and he does.

I took it down to Stoll's office, sent in my card and was admitted.[15] A man said he'd read it, thought it 'A1' and gave me an audition for one night at the Empire, Stratford. We got a girl and a good singer to rehearse and on the off-chance of an engagement, I went down with them, held the book and worked the curtain. It went like a roar. After the show, the manager came to me and said: 'You've got a winner there. I'll write and tell the office how well it was received.'

As I had heard nothing after three days, I went to Stoll's again and said I hoped they'd heard how well the sketch had gone. Heard nothing.

'But the manager said he would write and tell …'

'The damned fellow went off that night with all the takings.'

Then? 'Nothing doing. You've had your chance. Good morning.'

Later I sent the sketch to Courtice Pounds, the tenor of musical comedy fame.[16] He said he liked it immensely and would write immediately he returned from Berlin. He returned … but before arrangements could be made, he died. I was beginning to feel like a Jonah!

Bernhardt was playing Hugo's *Angelo* in Paris with, of course, great success.[17] Here, thought I, is the very thing for Mrs Patrick Campbell - she would *love* to challenge the Divine Sarah. I made an English version of it and, through some rich Jewish contacts, was invited to meet one of the famous Shubert brothers – the American theatrical producers. Samuel S Shubert had come over from America looking for plays to put on at the Waldorf (a new theatre just built).[18]

I went to dinner – champagne, all the usual bit – and Shubert regaled us with stories of his life: shoe-shine boy, programme seller etc. It was all rather touching. After dinner I read him the play. A conditional contract was written out, Mrs Pat to be engaged and all the rest of it. 'Of course,' he said, 'my brothers must endorse this, but they've given me a free hand. It's a cert all right.' He was going home the

---

[14] George Power (b. 1868), Irish actor and singer, also known as Littledale Power. His brother was Tyrone Power Senior (1869–1931), stage and screen actor, long in America.
[15] The theatre empire founded by Sir Oswald Stoll which merged in 1898 with that of one of his competitors, Edward Moss, to become Stoll Moss Theatres.
[16] Charles Courtice Pounds (1862–1927), leading tenor in the D'Oyly Carte company.
[17] *Angelo* by Victor Hugo (1835).
[18] Samuel S. Shubert (1878–1905), Polish-born American producer, writer and theatre manager.

following day and would send a contract to sign. He went back but, before he got to New York, he was killed in the dreadful Pennsylvania railway accident. The firm never took the Waldorf. [19]

In 1912, I wrote another original play, *Kynaston's Wife*. I read it to GA. 'Now, Winifred, you've done it!' He was under contract three productions ahead and couldn't make me an offer but he very generously said he'd give me the theatre for a charity matinée which I would produce myself.

What a chance! And what a problem. I had to raise some capital and it was some months before I saw my way. I met a man (let's call him Mr X) who wanted to get a venue for a one-act play to show off his fiancée (an actress) as a dancer. She was to play Columbine and he would put up the money, but he couldn't get a theatre. Another man – a friend of his – said his sister worked among the outcasts on the Thames Embankment in conjunction with the Chaplain of the Royal Savoy Chapel. Here was a charity for the matinée! I told them I would get the St James's. They hooted at such a boast. I said I would get it in writing but on my terms: I supplied the theatre and a four-act play of my own; Mr X must sign a contract to pay salaries and all expenses, placing £500 in a bank as guarantee. They opined that I wasn't asking for much, but agreed.

With GA, I arranged a vacant date and booked the St James's. We rehearsed in a room in the Strand. Clive Brook, an outstanding producer, was engaged, with a first-rate cast of London actors.[20] The bills went out in tube lifts etc. and everything promised to be perfect. The company believed in the play and loved their parts – it was roses, roses all the way ... only one week to the production.

Before that week was out, the *Titanic* went down at sea and that catastrophe killed the matinée – it had to be postponed. GA came up trumps and gave me another date, a week later to the day. But that very day was chosen by the profession to give a 'monster matinée' at Drury Lane on behalf of the *Titanic* victims and their families.[21]

There was no putting off our matinée a second time. It was heartbreak. We played to a thin house, no press present, everything a flop except the play itself. It was enthusiastically received (and, mind, I had no friends in front). GA and his wife occupied a box and when I was 'called', he led me himself to take my bow. The proceeds only covered expenses of scenery, stage-hands, advertising etc.

The artistes never received a penny of their fees – Mr X's cheques were all returned – duds. He was a bankrupt! The only 'pro' who got his fee (£70) was Clive Brook. From hearsay, three different theatres offered to take the play if I would contribute £500. That should have been Mr X's job. Of course no stigma was attached to me, and my standing in the profession was too well-known for the affair

---

[19] Samuel Shubert was fatally injured when the train in which he was travelling collided with several goods wagons loaded with dynamite in south Harrisburg, Pennsylvania, in 1905. A theatre in New York City is named after him. The Waldorf Theatre referred to here is not the one in New York City - which didn't open until 1926 - but the one in the Aldwych, London, now called the Novello. It opened on 22 May 1905 with an Italian opera, in spite of Shubert's death about a week earlier. The *New York Times* of that date referred to it as 'the Shuberts' London theatre'. It appears that Jacob Shubert (Samuel's brother) remained the lessee until July 1907 when he faced a London court over unpaid rent. It was said in court that he wanted nothing more to do with the Waldorf and, in fact, had already returned to the United States. (*New York Times*, 22 May 1905 and 27 July 1907).

[20] Clive Brook (1887–1974), actor and producer. James Kynaston was played by Lionel Atwill (1885–1946), a British stage actor who later made his name in horror films in the 1930s.

[21] The 'Dramatic and Operatic Matinée' in aid of the *Titanic* disaster fund took place at the Royal Opera House, Covent Garden on 14 May 1912. Among those appearing were Sarah Bernhardt, Anna Pavlova and Clara Butt. The souvenir programme included the first publication of Thomas Hardy's poem on the loss of the ship, 'The Convergence of the Twain.' Geoffrey Harvey, *The Complete Critical Guide to Thomas Hardy*, (London: Routledge, 2003), 47.

to injure me, but to be connected in any way to such a disgraceful fiasco was the most bitter trial I have ever faced in my life. GA was delighted with the production – 'in every way worthy of the St James's,' he said. A footnote to this story: the delinquent Mr X gave his life for his country in the Great War. For this and his family's sake, I do not disclose his name.

I mentioned much earlier that I had written a play especially for Mrs Kendal, *The Melcombe Marriage*.[22] She accepted it, produced it at Brighton and then suddenly left the stage. No public announcement or farewell performance. The Kendals! It was incredible. They sent me back the script – my royalties had brought me in precisely £26. Later it was explained to me what had happened. The Kendals had been accustomed to terms of seventy-eight per cent of the receipts per night but had ceased to draw houses which warranted such a high figure – sometimes it could not be met except at a loss. So all the country's managers agreed to make a stand and offer fifty per cent per night. The Kendals just folded their tents and stole away. I wouldn't have let them have my play if I had known. Yes, Mr Clement Scott, the stage is a gamble. I knew it before; I know it even better now.

Months later, I heard that a man called Arthur had taken one of the new theatres cropping up – the Duchess at Notting Hill Gate. Marion Terry was to be the leading lady. I sent her *The Melcombe Marriage* to read and asked her if she would play in it. She was delighted with the part and said yes. So-armed, I sent it to Mr Arthur telling him Miss Terry's opinion of it. In due course he sent for me.

When I arrived, he was otherwise engaged and his acting manager chatted with me. He told me Mr Arthur would take my play. He was having a meeting with his syndicate at that moment. It was evidently a stormy meeting – we could overhear angry voices. After a while, a message came: could Miss Dolan call again tomorrow, as Mr Arthur was so inopportunely detained. I left. That night, Arthur shot himself. Poor Marion – it was worse for her than for me – indeed, I was becoming quite acclimatised to it by now.

Kynaston's Wife was produced just once more – on 28 February 1921 at the Shaftesbury Theatre.[23] The Duke of York was in the Royal Box, Marshal Foch was there and all round the Dress Circle were the ambassadors from Spain, Belgium, Japan, Italy, Brazil and Poland.[24] The matinée was in aid of Lord Haig's Association and it made a lot of money.[25] It was not so expertly played as last time, but it went well. Of course by now it was rather old-fashioned – *Chu Chin Chow* was all the rage.[26]

---

[22] *The Stage Year Book* of 1908, reviewing the previous twelve months, said it could not have been said to have been a year 'of much vital achievement or distinction'. However, it referred to 'various interesting productions taking place in the provinces (…) such as *The Melcombe Marriage* by Miss Winifred Dolan, given by the Kendals'. Supporting the Kendals in this three-act play staged at the Theatre Royal, Brighton, in February 1907 was a cast of 11, including Bassett Roe and the Australian actress, Marie Lohr. L. Carson (ed.), *The Stage Year Book* of 1908 (London: Carson & Comerford, 1908).

[23] On the posters for the ill-fated St James's matinée of *Kynaston's Wife*, the playwright was billed as 'Rothwell Haig'. Winifred Dolan evidently used this name (derived from an area of West Yorkshire) as a male pseudonym to try to make progress in the field. By the charity performance of 1921, she had clearly decided to take the credit herself.

[24] Marshal Ferdinand Foch (1851–1929), French soldier and author.

[25] After finishing his active service, Field Marshal Douglas Haig, 1st Earl Haig (1861–1928), devoted his life to the welfare of ex-servicemen, travelling throughout the British Empire to promote their interests.

[26] *Chu Chin Chow* by Oscar Asche with music by Frederic Norton (1916). This musical comedy, based on the tale of *Ali Baba and the Forty Thieves*, opened at His Majesty's Theatre in August 1916 with Asche in the title role. It ran for five years and 2,235 performances. 'It inaugurated the concept of the long-running West End musical. Asche kept revising the show during its run, adding scenes and creating increasingly spectacular sets as a means of getting people who had already seen the show to come and experience it again and again.' William A. Everett and Paul R. Laird, (eds.), *The Cambridge Companion to the Musical*, (Cambridge: Cambridge University Press, 2008), 84.

Chapter X

'There's place and means for every man alive'
All's Well That Ends Well

The year of Queen Victoria's Diamond Jubilee (1897) was a bad one to be out of an engagement. There was no part for me in *The Princess and the Butterfly* at the St James's, so it was imperative to find some sort of work elsewhere.[1]

There was a Jubilee exhibition at West Kensington, organised by Imre Kiralfy.[2] I applied there and was directed to approach Miss McKenzie, who was head organiser of the women's section. She engaged me at once and we became great friends. She gave me a section to myself: 'Victorian Novelists'. Experience of every kind is always valuable so I felt I was in luck and the pay was good. I had to assemble first editions of all the said novelists and be on hand to answer enquiries from visitors. It meant a round of all the publishing houses and they were most helpful. I got an insight into yet another world. It was fun, too, to have the run of the exhibition itself.

This carried me over until September when GA offered me a part in his new play, *The Tree of Knowledge*.[3] So I was back again at the old theatre in a part I was to *create* this time – the first since *Midsummer Day*. The author was R. C. Carton who wrote *Liberty Hall*. It had a strong melodramatic flavour and did not carry the charm of the other play. I went into rehearsal and it turned out to be a low comedy role, flitting through all the acts with George Shelton as my n'er-do-well father.[4] They were not parts to afford either of us much chance – the humour lay in situation rather than in 'telling' lines of dialogue. Still, it was something quite different from what GA had given me before.

Julia Neilson played the adventuress to perfection and Harry Irving joined us to make a hit of the part of Roupelle.[5] Fay Davis was most charming as the girl GA marries. My role was to be a good-natured rough maid-of-all-work at the cottage. My father was a poacher and hanger-on, always stealing the port from the decanter on the sideboard – as I said, rather low comedy. But George Shelton was a splendid character actor and could make bricks without straw.

We opened in the play on 25 October 1897, and it ran for four months – that was 128 performances, not counting the Crystal Palace and Brighton matinees and

---

[1] *The Princess and the Butterfly* by Arthur Wing Pinero (1897).
[2] Imre Kiralfy (1845–1919), Austro-Hungarian impresario specialising in exhibitions. He set up London Exhibitions Ltd. in 1895 and staged a show at Earl's Court every year until 1907. The one in 1897 was called 'The Victorian Era'.
[3] *The Tree of Knowledge* by R.C.Carton (1897). 'A sub-Pinero problem play with an Eve whose present is just as lurid as her past.' George Rowell, *Theatre in the Age of Irving* (Oxford: Basil Blackwell, 1981), 125. The critic William Archer found it 'thoroughly interesting and entertaining. Other dramatists may be more terse, more eloquent or more scrupulously natural than Mr Carton, but no-one, to my thinking, writes more gracefully than he.' *The Theatrical World of 1897* (London: Walter Scott, 1898), 300. *The Tree of Knowl*edge went to Broadway and was also made into a film in 1920.
[4] George Shelton (1852–1932), English actor.

203

MISS WINIFRED DOLAN AND MR. GEORGE SHELTON.

Deborah.—"Oh! father!"
Sweadle.—"Oh! father! Wot d'ye mean by 'Oh! father?' I 'avent touched nothink."

15. Winifred Dolan in *The Tree of Knowledge*, by R. C. Carton, 1897, opposite George Shelton. 'My role was to be a good-natured rough maid-of-all-work at the cottage.'

the Grand Tour in the autumn. That brought it up to 160 – a good average run for a play in those days – certainly not a failure.

Here are the notices I got in the press:

> There's not a character in the piece that is not to be dwelt on with pleasure down to the loafing, poaching, sponging, do-nothing working man of Mr George Shelton and his ungainly but good-natured daughter in the person of Miss Winifred Dolan – *The Times*

> Miss Winifred Dolan as a rustic hand-maiden stood out with bold effect – *Daily Telegraph*

> Miss Winifred Dolan exhibits a great skill in the way she contrives to score in a tiny part from which she extracts every possible ounce of value – *Sporting Times*

When you look at the photograph, you might wonder why I was made up like that. I should explain that 'buns' were all the go with girls of that class at the time.

In February 1898, GA put on *Much Ado About Nothing* with Julia Neilson as Beatrice. I got the small part – much cut – of Margaret. It was a lovely production scenically and it must have been a terrible ordeal for Julia to play Beatrice after her sister-in-law, Ellen Terry, especially as Ellen came one night to see her in the part. It would be grossly unfair to offer comparison in such a case. It only ran for six weeks, and GA must have lost heavily on it as the décor and dresses designed by Graham Robertson must have been treble the expense of any modern play.[6] So on 4 April, I was out of a job again, but I had been earning for six months. Not bad.

The next production was a French Revolution play called *The Conquerors*[7] and while it was in rehearsal, GA asked me to take over the front of house as his acting manager had been taken ill. Behold me now – another unexpected guise! At night I had to be in evening dress and if any important personage came, I had to look after their comfort and so on.

One night, GA came through the slips to me between acts and said: 'Come along, the Countess of Shrewsbury is in Box A. I can't attend to her and she is alone.' He took me to the box and introduced me saying: 'Here's a co-religionist of yours, Lady Shrewsbury,' and then I realised she was the wife of the Lord Shrewsbury who was the patron of Pugin.[8] She was very charming and we had a nice little talk. I saw she got coffee and I then withdrew.

---

[5] Harry Brodribb Irving, (1870–1919), English actor, eldest son of Sir Henry Irving. He studied law at Oxford and was called to the Bar in 1894, but decided to pursue an acting career under the stage name H.B.Irving. He became one of the most prominent of the young English actors of the time and later established his own touring company. He returned to law during the First World War and wrote a celebrated work, *A Book of Remarkable Criminals* (Cassell 1918), a study of ten infamous characters, their crimes and subsequent court cases.

[6] Walford Graham Robertson (1866–1948), British painter, illustrator and costume designer. Some critics found the production 'overpowering in its elaboration'; the embellishments tending to stifle the play's liveliness'. (*Era*, 19 February 1898; *St James's Gazette*, 17 February 1898). Even the designer, Robertson, had doubts: 'It was magnificent, but *Much Ado About Nothing* ought not to be magnificent, but merely bright, sunny, gay. A glimpse of blue sky and a lick of distemper would have better suggested the atmosphere.' (*Time Was*, 264) Reviews from John F Cox (ed.), *Shakespeare in Production: Much Ado About Nothing* (Cambridge: Cambridge University Press, 1997), 44.

[7] *The Conquerors* by Paul Potter (1898).

[8] Augustus Welby Northmore Pugin (1812–1852), British architect most famous for his work on churches and the Houses of Parliament, and identified with the Gothic revival. John Talbot, the 16th Earl of Shrewsbury (1791–1852) was the supporter and benefactor of Pugin, but his wife, Maria Theresa, died in 1856. The lady in the St James's box in 1898 must have been a later countess.

16. A studio portrait of Winifred Dolan in costume as Margaret in the lavish
production of *Much Ado About Nothing*, presented at the St James's in 1898.
George Alexander played Benedick opposite Julia Neilson's Beatrice
(Alexander Corbett/Alfred Ellis/National Archives)

That was the sort of thing an acting manager was called upon to do at night
– the rest of his work is the business side of running a theatre from the office – worse
than my job as a secretary: a dog's life to my mind. I was glad when the sick man
came back. But it was another experience. This play also ran for only six weeks.

They say that one failure will eat up the profits of three successes in the
theatre. What a gamble the whole thing is! The new play, *The Ambassador*, was the
first by Mrs Craigie who, as John Oliver Hobbes, was the famous novelist.[9] GA
gave me the part of the nun. I opened the play with Fay Davis, but did not appear
any more, although under a fake name in the programme I had a small part later
among some 'guests'.

When we played at the usual flying matinée at Brighton, we had an

---

[9] *The Ambassador*, a comedy in four acts by John Oliver Hobbes [Pearl Craigie] (1898). The playwright had, in fact,
had one earlier piece performed on the stage: *Journeys End in Lovers' Meeting*, described as a 'one-act proverb',
featuring Ellen Terry in 1894. The Pearl Mary Teresa Craigie papers, New York Library for the Performing Arts.

experience that was at once dangerous and amusing. The Theatre Royal was old and the doors in the flats were still cut out of the frame, leaving a sill of about two-and-half inches to step over. In London doors we now had flat sills of iron, so we were not on our guard about this pitfall.

I was the first to stumble over the thing, but quickly recovered myself. GA was standing ready to follow me and I tried to attract his attention to the floor hoping his eye would catch sight of the trap. Alas, he could not understand me. On he came, stumbling far worse than I had and clutching at a table to recover his balance. There was an ominous titter.

Fred Terry was due to enter next and we *both* started trying to telegraph an SOS to him. He shook his head, bewildered. On he came, a big heavy man, six feet tall, and promptly measured his whole length on the floor. The house howled with delight, for by now they had foreseen what might happen. As for us on the stage, we were convulsed.

The play was an enormous success. Produced on 2 June 1898, it ran for eighteen months. Mrs Craigie was a convert and said nice things about my nun. She was a most fascinating woman with the brain of a man, the intuition of a woman and the wit of an educated American. We all loved her. She died young at the height of her powers.

I never played at the St James's again: I got engagements, of sorts, at the Court, Criterion, Avenue and Terry's and also played in another charity matinée at the Haymarket. Why did I not enjoy wider success? Well, one of the difficulties as a 'lone wolf' on the stage was that, not belonging to any theatrical family and, as a woman, unable to drink in bars, I never knew of a coming production until I read of it in the *Daily Telegraph*. By that time it was probably cast; my only chance would be as an understudy.

I remember when Tree was announced as presenting a new play called *The Darling of the Gods*, I rushed off to Her Majesty's and was lucky enough to run into him in the foyer.[10] His acting manager was with him. 'Any chance of a small part for me, Mr Tree?' Turning to his man, he said: 'If only we'd waited! She's just what we wanted.' Then, to me: 'It's a small part but an important one and we couldn't find exactly what we wanted. I have just signed a contract with a girl because we couldn't wait any longer.'

I read that Bourchier and Boucicault at the Criterion were doing a new play by R. C. Carton, so I wrote to the playwright asking for a part. He wrote back: 'All parts filled. Tell them to give you an understudy.' I went down to the Criterion and was engaged at once to understudy Miss Compton (lead and author's wife),[11] as well as an elderly spinster aunt and a kitchen maid with adenoids. It had a long run and reimbursed my exchequer.

There were understudy rehearsals three times a week for several weeks and 'refreshers' from time to time. Boucicault would sometimes come himself and take a hand. This was something like the stage as I had pictured it. I was called at the last moment to play the spinster aunt. Dear old Fanny Coleman played her and she had not turned up for the matinée. The week before that, there had been no matinée because it was Derby Day. When Miss C. turned up at night she said she thought all matinées had been taken off. A bit of luck for me. I got all my laughs and they were very pleased with me.

---

[10] *The Darling of the Gods* by David Belasco and John Luther Long (1903).
[11] Katherine Compton (1853–1928), English actress.

In 1901, 1902 and 1903, I got four engagements, including the one mentioned above. One was as a housekeeper in a *lever de rideau* on the same bill as a play called *The Lion Hunter*.[12] One Saturday matinée, the girl who was playing the chief lady of the group of lion hunters fell and sprained her ankle. No understudies had been given out and the wretched man who was stage-managing was in a mortal funk – it meant dismissal.

He called all the ladies, including me, on to the stage and implored one of us to save him by *reading* the part that night. They all refused – 'never done such a thing, would die of fright' etc – so I got up and said: 'Send out for a dozen oysters and a bottle of stout, shut me up in the star room, keep the cleaners off the stairs and I'll *play* the part tonight.' I had three hours to learn it, dress and make up.

I played it that night and was, though I say it myself, word perfect. There were only three acts. The SM wept when he thanked me and no-one knew of his lapse. It taught him a lesson. Harry Irving was in the cast and he told the producer that he should let me keep the part, but the injured girl was under contract for the run. Besides, she was back on the Monday, limping.

It had been an unusual experience – and, incidentally, was the last part I ever played on a public stage.

---

[12] *The Lion Hunter* by J.T.Grein and Martha Leonard , Imperial Theatre, 1901.

Chapter XI

'Why, man, he doth bestride the narrow world like a Colossus ...'
– Julius Caesar

Before I move to the conclusion of my story, I want to dwell here awhile and offer a few thoughts on the greatest theatrical partnership of the time: Irving and Terry. On 13 October 1905, Irving played Becket at Bradford. The last words he ever spoke – on stage and in life, it seems – were: 'Into thy hands, O Lord, into thy hands.' He became ill shortly afterwards, was taken into his hotel and in a few minutes he was dead.

I was fortunate enough to be present at his funeral at Westminster Abbey. It came about because I'd run into Harry Irving in the street. 'Of course, you're coming?' he said. 'I? My dear, I am nobody!' I exclaimed. He gave me a ticket there and then. Dear Harry – he died young, but left a son to carry on the name.[1]

Irving was not only a very great actor, he was a very great man. He would have been great in any walk of life – as a churchman, statesman, barrister or scholar. He combined in his essence a curious blend of the satanic and the saintly, *vide* his Iachimo, Iago, Becket and the Vicar of Wakefield. Dare I say he seemed to possess both potentialities in his make-up?

His charity was a by-word, his hand was never out of his pocket. He raised the status of his profession: great artists such as Alma-Tadema and Burne-Jones were proud to design his productions,[2] and great musicians such as Sullivan and Edward German were proud to write his incidental music.[3] To his famous suppers at the Beefsteak Club came Bernhardt, Duse, Coquelin, Liszt, Paderewski and other leading lights of literature, law, politics and art in all its forms.[4]

---

[1] Laurence Irving (1897–1988), H.B. Irving's son. He was a costume and scenery designer on the London stage in the 1920s before moving into the film industry, in which he became a set designer, art director and co-producer. His career is recounted in his *Designing for the movies: the Memoirs of Laurence Irving*, (Reprinted by Scarecrow Press 2005). Laurence Irving was also the author of a biography of his grandfather, *Henry Irving, the Actor and his World* (New York: Macmillan, 1952).'It remains the definitive account of Irving's life in all its aspects.' (John H.B. Irving [Laurence's son], the Henry Irving Foundation, www.henryirving.co.uk).

[2] Sir Lawrence Alma-Tadema (1836–1912), Dutch-born artist, who settled in London in 1870, and Sir Edward Burne-Jones (1833–1898), leading British artist and designer and member of the pre-Raphaelite group. Early generations of scene-painters had left the theatre in pursuit of academic respectability, but Irving's reputation, and the growing respectability of the theatre, encouraged Alma-Tadema to prepare designs for his *Cymbeline* (1896) and *Coriolanus* (1901). Edward Burne-Jones designed his *King Arthur* (1895). These designs were then painted by Hawes Craven, Irving's principal scenic artist, and Joseph Harker. Joseph Donohue (ed.), *The Cambridge History of British Theatre:1660 to 1895* (Cambridge: Cambridge University Press, 2004), 322.

[3] Sir Edward German (1862–1936), British musician and composer, best known for his operettas *Merrie England* (1902) and *Tom Jones* (1907). Irving had admired German's score for the production of Richard III in 1889, staged by the American actor-manager, Richard Mansfield, and hired him for his Henry VIII in 1892. After that, ' (…) his position in the firmament was confirmed (….) the set of Three Dances from this became extremely popular and were the first pieces to explore the distinctive 'Olde English' style, a species of musical mock Tudor with which German came to be particularly associated.' David Russell Hulme, *Orpheus with his lute: sources of Edward German's music for the Victorian and Edwardian drama*, 2000, as reprinted on the Sir Edward German Library, **www.edwardgerman.org**).

[4] Franz Liszt, (1811-1886), Hungarian composer, pianist and teacher. Ignacy Jan Paderewski (1860-1941), Polish pianist and composer, later Prime Minister of Poland.

His list of honours – English and American – occupied lines after his name. He was the first actor to be knighted. His country gave him burial among the great dead in Westminster Abbey. His name will have a place for all time in English annals as an actor and as a man.

The old-time player, instead of calling himself an actor, would say proudly he belonged to the Profession – with a capital P. Did not Irving bid me: 'Uphold the honour of the Profession'? The term had been a source of ridicule for years but I think actors clung to it as a fierce rejection of the dictum expressed by many that acting was not art because, supposedly, it was not a *creative* art. All that has changed now, thanks to Irving. Does not the actor give the dramatist creations of his brain, of life? Would these see light of day if the actor did not bring them to birth by his art?

The decadent phase through which the stage passed during the First World War soon passed away. The decline of the actor-manager cleared the way for the producer. A new era dawned: repertory companies supplied the training for a new race of players. The English people have become drama-conscious again and actors no longer play to an elite but to the public at large, whose servants they are and by whose favour alone the drama can live. This is all to the good and a healthy sign. Stage history bears witness to the fact that when the general level of acting is very high, no giant appears, but when the level sinks, a Man of the Hour always arises: a Kean, a Garrick or an Irving.[5] Is there anyone alive on the stage who can compare with them? Certainly not. But look at the galaxy of talent presented by John Gielgud (Ellen Terry's great nephew), Donald Wolfit, Laurence Olivier, the Thorndikes, Edith Evans etc. Or the crowd of dramatists of the first order, male and female. There is room and opportunity for everyone and anyone to shine, given the necessary qualifications.

So to Ophelia. Had I lost touch with her? No. The final photograph she signed for me was of her as Volumnia in *Coriolanus*, the last part she ever played with Irving at the Lyceum. On it she wrote 'Affectionately, Ellen Terry'. It is not dated, but the year was 1903.[6]

Was she a great actress? Yes, a very great actress in high comedy, compounded of laughter and tears. She was incapable of failure in any part: she was not Lady Macbeth according to the Siddons tradition, for she was not a tragic actress, but she achieved a tour de force by presenting the character on other (but perfectly legitimate) lines. Anyone who goes to see her picture by Sargent in the Tate Gallery in this role would exclaim at once: 'Ha! Lady Macbeth, of course!' without referring to any catalogue.[7]

Something of Ellen Terry, it seems, overflowed in every part and remained 'unacted'. And thus, while other players are remembered because they were Hamlet or Phèdre or Cleopatra, Ellen Terry is remembered because she was Ellen Terry. That is perfect. She was incomparable and unique.

---

[5] Edmund Kean (1789–1833), considered to be the greatest English actor of his time and David Garrick (1717–1789), actor, playwright, theatre manager and producer – one of the greatest figures in English theatre in the 18th century. Biographies of Kean include Barry Cornwall, *The Life of Edmund Kean,* (London: Edward Moxon, 1835, reprinted US: Kessinger Publishing, 2007); and of Garrick, Percy Fitzgerald, *The Life of David Garrick*, (London: Tinsley Brothers, 1868, reprinted US:BiblioBazaar, 2008).

[6] 1903 may have been the year Winifred Dolan was given the signed photograph, but Irving's *Coriolanus*, with Ellen Terry as Volumnia, had been staged two years earlier – at the Lyceum in April, 1901.

[7] The painting is *Ellen Terry as Lady Macbeth*, oil on canvas, 1889, by John Singer Sargent (American 1856–1925), presented to the Tate Gallery by Sir Joseph Duveen in 1906. Ellen Terry approved of the work. In her diary in 1888 she wrote: 'The picture of me is nearly finished and I think it is magnificent.' Ellen Terry, *The Story of My Life* (1908), 263.

John Gielgud wrote of her: 'Ellen Terry could discover no author to fit her genius – even with Shaw and Barrie to find plays for her – and, in a noble effort to move with the times, she chose a play of Ibsen's which did not suit her. But the public would have none of it and she was forced to revive *Much Ado About Nothing* to restore her losses.'

She ended her active life by lecturing on Shakespeare and giving excerpts from the plays in England and America. But to the very end, whenever an audience saw her entering a box at the theatre, they would give her an ovation.

After her marriage to James Carew in America in 1907 – a man younger than her own children![8] – a break with old associations of the past inevitably followed: she was starting a new life. It was one of those unaccountable happenings – not uncommon in life – a sort of reawakening of a second spring, fated to know no summer.

---

[8] James Carew was the leading man in Ellen Terry's American tour of 1907. When they married in Pittsburgh, she was 60 and he was 31. The marriage lasted only two years, though they remained on good terms.

Chapter XII

'Our revels now are ended'
– The Tempest

When I sat, as an eighteen-year-old, in the Grand Theatre in Leeds in 1886 marvelling at Irving in *Faust*, little did I imagine how much my life would become entwined with the man playing the title role in that production, George Alexander. GA and Herbert Beerbohm Tree were rivals and in the long run, I think Tree beat him. In the early days, the St James's was dubbed the Comedie-Française of England. Later, Tree's Her Majesty's became the premier theatre – always excepting the Lyceum, of course, because it stood alone.

One night, GA came by in his brougham and picked me up.[1] In the course of conversation, he said to me: 'Do you know why I make money and Tree does not?' 'No,' I lied politely though I had my own idea. 'Tell me why.'

'I produce plays from the office – he produces them from the stage.'

Exactly. Tree was an artist and a very great character actor. GA was a hard-boiled businessman.

With a handsome face, charm of manner (out of business hours) and a genius at taking the public pulse, he became a matinée idol as the phrase went. When he stepped out of that frame, he failed. How astute it was of him to cast his early productions with such aristocratic names on the programmes and bills – Nutcombe Gould, Vane Tempest and Lady Monckton, for instance.[2] They secured him a society following to fill his stalls![3] After his position was secured, he discarded them and fell back on 'real' actors. Towards the end – long after I had left him – he took to producing rubbishy American plays.

When Wilde crashed, two of his plays were running, one at the Criterion and the other, *The Importance of Being Earnest*, at the St James's.[4] Wyndham had the

---

[1] Brougham: a four-wheeled, horse-drawn carriage.

[2] James Nutcombe Gould (1849–1899), English actor, the son of a wealthy rector and the brother of a diplomat; Francis Adolphus Vane-Tempest (1863–1932), English actor who came from a line of senior military figures and himself had been an army major.

[3] 'Victorian and Edwardian audiences were so diverse that it is impossible to consider a generic audience for this period.' Jim Davis and Victor Emeljanow, *Victorian and Edwardian audiences*, *The Cambridge Companion to Victorian and Edwardian Theatre*, Kerry Powell (ed.), (Cambridge: Cambridge University Press 2004), 93. Further light on this subject is offered by Cary M. Mazer: 'Audiences in even the most fashionable theatres [in London] included members of every class, from aristocrats and financiers, to businessmen and professionals, to shopkeepers, clerks, and artisans, to servants and labourers. The lower classes had their own seating areas, with their own entrances, lobbies, bars, and lavatories in the theatre. But, in the more expensive parts of the house, the auditorium was by no means as segregated as members of 'society' might wish. After all, not everyone could be admitted to a fashionable drawing-room, but anyone who could afford the higher-priced ticket and had the right clothing could sit in the stalls or the dress circle.' (On-line essay, *Wilde, Society and Society Drama*, 1993, www.english.upenn.edu/~cmazer).

[4] *The Importance of Being Earnest* opened at the St James's on 14 February 1895. Joseph Donohue notes that the copy-text for the first edition, with annotations in Oscar Wilde's hand, was typed by Winifred Dolan; Donohue (ed), *Oscar Wilde's The Importance of Being Earnest. A Reconstructive Edition* (Gerrards Cross: Colin Smythe, 1995), 20, 81-4.

decency to forgo his profits and withdraw the play. GA just pasted a broad red band through the author's name on all his bills and programmes and continued to reap the boom attached to the sensation caused by poor Wilde's downfall.

I used often at first to feel sore at the way GA used me for jobs that he wouldn't have got anyone else to accept. It took me some time to realise there was no philanthropy in business. Of course I suited the purpose and he was right in considering I had a quid pro quo in the exclusive and varied chances of experience he gave me. It was he who recommended me to the Glasgow and the other amateurs from whom I got well-paid engagements.

Consider, too, how he let me read all my plays to him – an unheard of favour – and gave me his theatre to produce one. He was genuinely fond of me and though I could never feel his attraction, I was deeply grateful to him. He died in 1918 worth £100,000. Tree died a few years later – bankrupt. But it is Tree's name that will live. Tree was a great wit like his brother, Max Beerbohm.[5] When Oscar Asche produced *Chu Chin Chow* during the 1914–18 war, the scene in the slave market exhibited a degree of nudity that stretched even the 'new morality' of the British public to snapping point. Asche invited Tree to come and see it. After the performance, he said to his guest: 'Well, Tree, what do you think of *that* for spectacle?' 'Rather more navel than millinery,' was Tree's laconic reaction to the scanty costumes.

A propos of nudity on the stage. When the death of Edward VII in 1910 ushered in a new Georgian period, the cry was beginning to be 'back to nature', together with the jibe that 'to the pure, all things are impure'.

Christian modesty was not outraged in malice; it was simply unknown territory. And the stage, of its very nature, always reflects the age. In *The Gay Lord Quex*, the lady undresses to the last shred of decency in full sight of the audience in the Great Bedroom Scene.[6] It is true that Irene Vanbrugh played the part and must, by her delicacy of touch, have robbed it of provocative tendency. But that the charming daughter of a Dean of Exeter Cathedral did play it was a sign of the times.[7] As Ellen Terry said in her autobiography: 'Any suggestions of indelicacy in my treatment of a part always blighted me.'[8]

One more comment before I end my story: salaries. Money then had much greater value than it does today: £1 meant £1. The only salaries at the top I knew of for certain were Ellen Terry's, Marion Terry's and Fred Terry's (with his wife, Julia Neilson). Ellen drew the fabulous sum of £100 a week; Marion £40; Fred and Julia £50 each when they played together. The 'rank and file' were on anything from £3–£30 for established players. I had reached £7.

After my last engagement at Terry's in the Strand came to an end, 1903 was drawing to a close. I sat down to face the future, for the past three years had not been encouraging and I felt I had reached the point when a decision had to be made. I was 35 years old. As far as I knew (though kind providence arranged otherwise) I would have to earn my living for the rest of my life. Luckily I never looked my years, but

On 6 April, the day of Wilde's arrest on the charge of gross indecency, his name was removed from the programme and all advertising. The box office collapsed and the play closed on 8 May, having run for 83 performances. (V & A Theatre Collections, notes on the first stage production of *The Importance of Being Earnest*, **www.vam.ac.uk**). Wilde's *An Ideal Husband*, originally at the Haymarket, had opened at the Criterion on 13 April and was withdrawn on 27 April.

[5] Sir Henry Maximilian Beerbohm (1872–1956), English parodist and caricaturist.

[6] Pinero's comedy in four acts, The Gay Lord Quex, was first performed at the Globe Theatre in April 1899, with Irene Vanbrugh playing opposite Sir John Hare.

[7] As the daughters of the Dean of Exeter, Irene and Violet Vanbrugh were generally considered to be the first from a 'good' family to go on stage.

[8] *The Story of My Life*, by Ellen Terry (1908). Chapter VIII, 'Work at the Lyceum', 162.

if I were to make good permanently in some other walk of life, it was high time to set about it.

Of all the scores of girls in the companies I had been in, only two had lasted as long as myself. If 'new morality' plays were the stuff I would be called upon to play, what prospects were there for me? A touring life after my experiences with Otho Stuart under exceptional conditions of travel was not one I was prepared to enter into for the rest of my life. In a train with a crowd all day and not even Sundays free to attend to the thing that mattered.

Well then, what? The New Year of 1904 had hardly begun before I received three offers: From GA to replace Legge again as his secretary. Would I be permanent this time? Would my health stand the strain such as the six months I described – stand it for years? I refused. To go on tour at a very good salary as leading lady in *The Gay Lord Quex*. No! The Secretaryship of the head office in London of the Women's Unionist Association: £160 p.a.[9] What had I said to Clement Scott: 'I only want my chance.' I had had it. 'If I fail, I shall quit.' I accepted the offer. It took courage and nearly broke my heart.

If I failed – and I don't think I did altogether – I am inclined to wonder whether my line lay less in acting than producing. But, you see, I wasn't a man. Women now have come into their own – they can be doctors, barristers, MPs, soldiers, sailors, even clergy. More power to their elbow say I, who knew what it was to be a woman in the 1890s. I am now an old woman of 81. Looking back over more than 70 years, I am glad to have lived in such stirring times. For me, they were years of rich experience and testing endeavour. If you were to ask me whether I had any regrets about those 13 years on the stage, I would say: No, I wouldn't change one hour.

---

[9] One of the forerunners of the Conservative party's women's organisations. Dolan continued to write during her time with the Women's Unionist Association. She was the author of *The History of Social Reform During One Hundred Years* (London: Love & Malcomson, 1910) and *'Wake up, John Bull!' A political play in one act*, Lacy's Acting Edition of Plays, Vol. 162, (London: T. H. Lacy, 1912).

Editor's Epilogue

'I count myself in nothing else so happy as in a soul remembering my good friends'
– King Richard II

We left Winifred Dolan's story in 1904 as she was about to arrive at the Women's Unionist Association armed with the stamina, organisational prowess and impeccable typing skills that had been honed through ten years with the demanding George Alexander.

We can only surmise that she became a stalwart of the Association and an engaging colleague, regaling the rest of the staff with some of the anecdotes she related in her memoirs.

To catch up with her later life, we must jump forward some sixteen years and to a different place: New Hall at Boreham on the edge of Chelmsford in Essex. Here, the English Community of the Canonesses of the Holy Sepulchre had their school.

It will be clear from her story that, throughout her career, Winifred Dolan was careful to balance her deep religious conviction with her work as an actress – not always an easy task. Not for her a Sunday lie-in and special dispensation to attend later Mass after the Gospel!

To trace Winifred Dolan's path to the convent and school of New Hall, we have to go back to Chapter I of her story, to elder brother Martin Oswald ('Ossie') and big sister Mary Agnes ('Aggie'), her companions on those early trips to the Grand Theatre in Leeds. Ossie became a military chaplain in the Great War and afterwards a Canon of the Church in Sheffield. And in 1884, Aggie became a nun. Aggie's calling would, no doubt, have delighted Winifred, but it also presented problems. As Tony Tuckwell points out in his book *New Hall And Its School*, the Prioress at that time, Reverend Mother Aloysia Austin Butler, strongly disapproved of the acting profession and rather cruelly banned Winifred from visiting the convent to see her sister.

But fortune, which had so often deserted her in her acting career, came to smile on her. In 1918, Aggie, as Sister Aloysia Magdalen, was elected Prioress at New Hall and, in 1920, she braved the disapproval of some in the Community and invited Winifred to become a lay teacher of drama and elocution. It was a decision that was to have a profound impact.

With the sort of gusto she'd displayed all those years before at Leeds Girls' High School, Winifred set about founding what became a brilliant dramatic tradition at New Hall which lasts to this day. A Shakespeare play was presented every year in which she was the producer or leading lady – sometimes both. The stage in the 300-seat auditorium was reconstructed under her guidance to a design based on that of a West End theatre.

The English Community of the Canonesses of the Holy Sepulchre moved from New Hall in 2005, but continues to thrive elsewhere. Sister Mary Therese was one of those apprehensive young schoolgirls whose acting efforts came under the scrutiny of Miss Dolan during the school's wartime evacuation to Newnham Paddox near Rugby in Warwickshire. 'She was usually dressed in a suit jacket and trousers and she had a stick which she thumped on the floor - a little bit frightening, really,' said Sister Therese. 'But she convinced me of my part – she could really get you into the spirit of it. She was an amazing lady.'

Sister Stephanie was in the youngest class during the evacuation and recalls the production put on by Winifred Dolan for the tercentenary of the Community in 1942. 'We were taken along to Miss Dolan's room – a major event – to be grilled by her about our parts. We were in a circle on the floor, Miss Dolan would sit in her chair, in a rather masculine suit, close cropped hair and a deep strong voice, pointing her stick at you when it was your turn to deliver your line. We all trembled.'

Some years earlier, in July 1934, Winifred had taken on a particularly daunting project - writing, producing and acting in a pageant to celebrate the fiftieth anniversary of her sister's Profession of Vows. No expense was spared in the lavish telling of the history of New Hall from the time of its grant by Harold to the Canons of Waltham Abbey in 1062 to its occupation by the Canonesses who returned to England from Liege in Belgium in 1794, eventually arriving at New Hall in 1799. The second part celebrated in five tableaux the life of the Prioress from the time she received the call to the religious life.

The *Essex Chronicle* thought it all entrancingly lovely: 'Miss Dolan has earned high praise in the past, but now she has excelled herself. To write the play, produce it and act in it is a great achievement, especially when the work is as splendid as this. She is an artiste. There can be no higher tribute.' How Winifred would have liked that sort of review when she was at the St James's!

The Community lived a semi-enclosed life and Winifred was one of the first lay teachers. Her considerable experience of the 'outside world' often came in useful, for example at the 1931 general election. Tony Tuckwell explains in his book that this was the first at which the nuns were enfranchised and they were urged by the Church to use their vote.

Nearly all of them decided to go to Boreham School polling station and one nun described the occasion: 'It was a tremendous event as not only had most of the nuns never been in a car, but most had never left the Enclosure since their entrance years before. Miss Dolan was there to be our chaperone and to protect us against all aggressors. We were going very early so no-one should be at the voting booth to see us. Remember, a nun had never before been seen in Boreham and it was feared we might be mobbed.'

Winifred lived for many years in a cottage in the grounds of the convent and was evidently regarded by young nuns and school pupils with a mixture of affection and awe. On her return to New Hall after the war, she was no longer able to live on her own and the last twelve years of her life were spent in the Community infirmary. She died on 11 June 1958 and was buried in the Community cemetery. 'I have been glad and oh so grateful for the privilege to end my days in the peace and sanctuary of beloved New Hall,' she wrote shortly before her death.

She left behind at New Hall practically everything from her theatrical and teaching careers – annotated scripts, account books, programmes, production photographs, a hand-written manual on stage management, letters and pictures from Terry, Irving and others, her prized brooch from Queen Victoria and, of course, her memoirs.

The things that haven't survived are the plays she writes about in Chapter IX

17. The Dolan siblings: Mary Agnes ('Aggie'), Martin Oswald ('Ossie') and Winifred. This picture was probably taken around the time that Mary Agnes became Prioress of New Hall in 1918. **(New Hall archives)**

– *Octave's Eyes, The Showman, The Lion Cub, Kynaston's Wife* and so on. She put in her memoir: 'A few days ago, I burned all my plays, press notices etc. and said *finis* to the past.' Fortunately for us, not *all* her past.

Just under a year before Winifred's death, the lights went down for the last time at the St James's Theatre. It closed on 27 July 1957 under much protest and was demolished to make way for an office building. In the last months of its existence, a huge nationwide campaign, led by the actress Vivien Leigh, was fought to try to save this most popular of theatres. Sir Winston Churchill offered £500 to help start a fund to save the building. The issue was raised in the Houses of Parliament several times and there were marches in the street but there was to be no reprieve.

The demolition went ahead, the only concession to the campaigners being a new statement of policy by the London County Council indicating that, in future, no active theatre in London would be allowed to be demolished without a replacement being built.

Happily, the show goes on at the two other theatres that feature in Winifred Dolan's story. For an illustrated history of the Grand Theatre, Leeds, see Patricia Lennon and David Joy, *Grand Memories* (Ilkley: Great Northern Books, 2006). David Rankin's web-site dedicated to the history of the Theatre Royal, Margate is at www.trm-archive.blogspot.com

Editor's Note

The process of establishing accurate birth dates for theatre people of the nineteenth century has been a difficult one. The dates can vary by as much as five years either way depending on the reference book used. These are based broadly on two reliable sources: *Who's Who In The Theatre* (Pitman and Sons), compiled and edited at the turn of that century by John Parker, and *Stage Deaths 1850–1990*, compiled by George B. Bryan (Westport, Conn.: Greenwood Press). Thanks to both for the information. Details about actors and plays in performance are drawn from the 'Hand-Lists' of plays complied by Allardyce Nicoll in *A History of English Drama, 1660–1900*, Vol. V, *Late Nineteenth Century Drama, 1850–1900*, (Cambridge: Cambridge University Press, 1959), Donald Mullin, *Victorian Actors and Actresses in Review* (Westport, Conn.: Greenwood Press, 1983), and *Victorian Plays: A Record of Significant Productions on the London Stage, 1837–1901* (Westport, Conn.: Greenwood Press, 1987).

Index